There's an Answer for That

Lisa Payne

Copyright © 2018 by Lisa Payne All rights reserved.

No part of this book may be reproduced, or transmitted in any form or by any means, including photocopying, recording, or other electronic or mechanical methods, stored in a retrieval system, or transmitted in any form or by any means without the prior written permission of the publishers, author, except in the case of brief quotations embodied in reviews and certain other non-commercial uses permitted by copyright law.
Scripture quotations marked (KJV) are taken from the Holy Bible, King James Version.
       Lisa Payne
There's an Answer for That: Why Be Troubled Any Longer
    ISBN 978-0-578-85303-1

There's an Answer for That

Contents

Fornication Is A Sin	5-6
Cannot Serve Two Masters	7-8
How Can You Say You Love	9
Watch What You Love	10-11
Jesus is Lord	12-13
The Holy Ghost	14-18
Be Not Deceived	19-20
Presence of God	21-24
Man's True Identity	25-32
The Tongue	35-38
Don't Believe the Lie	39-52
Wake Up	53-55
Homosexuality/Lesbianism	56-57
What Is Faith??	58-60
What Is Fear??	61-69
Encouragement	70
Repentance	71-74
Consequences	75-77
Divination/Witchcraft	78-80
Consulting God	81-87
Lack of Knowledge	88-91
When Trouble Comes	92-100

Fornication Is A Sin

Did you know that **FORNICATION** is a sin???

This is not of God to be in a relationship and/or dating and you two are living together and are not married.
Or even to be sexually active with someone and you are not married to them… God honors marriage. It is important for us to learn the word of God, to see what is acceptable of the Lord?

Hebrews 13:4 "Marriage is honorable in all, and the Bed undefiled: but whoremongers and adulterers God will Judge." I Thessalonians 4:3-4 "For this is the will of God, even Your sanctification, that ye should abstain from fornication. That every one of you should know how to possess his vessel in sanctification and honor;"

I Corinthians 6:18-20 "Flee fornication. Every sin that a man doeth is without the body; but he that commiteth fornication sinneth against his own body. What?

Know ye not that your body is the temple of the Holy Ghost, which is in you which ye have of God, and ye are not your own? For ye are bought

With a price: therefore, glorify God in your body and in your spirit, which are God's" ……

Now society would have you think that it is ok to be intimate with someone before marriage. Please be not deceived, this is not correct. God is a holy God, and we saints are to be holy ourselves. If someone cannot wait till marriage to be intimate with you, then unfortunately, this is not love but lust. 1 Peter 1:15-16 "But as he which hath called you is holy, so be ye holy in all manner of conversation; because it is written, be ye holy; for I am holy." So please, respect your bodies which are God's bodies.

JESUS is Lord!!!!!!!!!!

Jesus loves you more than you know............

Cannot Serve Two Masters

St. Matthew 6:24 **No man can serve two masters**: for either he will hate the one and love the other; or else he will hold to the one and despise the other. Ye cannot serve God and mammon" ….

It is time to stop running. In life you must make a choice to live or die. With Jesus there is life eternal and with the devil, there is death….

Did you know that the wage of sin is death? Either death physically or spiritually cut off from the provisions of God. Let me just tell you, you do not want to be in this wicked world cut off from God's provisions.

Which will you choose? Be not deceived, you cannot go to church on Sunday and drink, fornicate, club and do all types of sin, Monday through Saturday, because then who are you really pacifying…. yourself perhaps, just to say you went to church. When you are walking with the Lord Jesus, it is all or nothing. Taste and see that the Lord is good. You do not have to live that way, there is a better way. This way is with Jesus. For he is soon to return, don't you want to be ready. Please get your house in order. To say you have the Lord in your life is to obey all his commandments and to keep his statues. How can you say you love the Lord whom you cannot see, but hate your brother whom you can see????? God is of love. He teaches us to love one another.

St. Matthew 5:44-46 "But I say unto you, Love your enemies, bless them that curse you, do good to them that hate you, and pray for them which despitefully use you, and persecute you; That ye may be the children of your Father which is in heaven: for he maketh his sun to rise on the evil and on the good, and sendeth rain on the just and on the unjust. For if ye love them which love you, what reward have ye? Do not even the publicans the same?"

There is a difference between the saved and unsaved.......... JESUS is Lord!!!!

<u>JESUS The Living Word!!!</u>

How Can You Say You Love God?

How can you say you love God whom you have not seen, yet hate your Brother whom you have seen?

1 John 4:7-8 "Beloved, let us love one another: for love is of God; and everyone that loveth is born of God, and knoweth God. He that loveth not knoweth not God; For God is love." St. John 15:12 "This is my commandment, that ye love one another, as I have loved You." St. Matthew 5:44-46 "But I say unto you, Love your enemies, bless them that curse you, do good to them that hate you, and pray for them which despitefully use you, and persecute you; That ye may be the children of your Father which is in heaven: for he maketh his sun to rise on the evil and on the good, and sendeth rain on the just and on the unjust. For if ye love them which love you, what reward have ye? Do not even the publicans the same?"

We must love one another with brotherly love through our Lord and Savior Jesus Christ. No one is perfect. We must judge ourselves so that we can help mankind and not live as hypocrites. This is not of God to fight among one another or to have strife, anger, resentment, jealousy, or bitterness with one another. Our God is a God of love, and we ought to be like him. God wants us to live in peace with all men. Please forgive others. Keep in mind that God loves us all and he will not force himself on no one. We are all born with free will. That means you are free to make decisions in your life.

St. Matthew 6:14-15 "For if ye forgive men their trespasses, your heavenly Father will also Forgive you: But if ye forgive not men their trespasses, neither will your Father forgive your trespasses. "

Jesus is soon to return......don't you want to be ready................

Watch What You Love

1 John 2:15-16 "**Love not the world, neither the things that are in the world. If any** Man loves the world; the love of the Father is not in him. For all that is in the world, the lust of the flesh, and the lust of the eyes, and the pride of life, is not of the Father, but is of the world."

I Timothy 6:8-11 "And having food and raiment let us be therewith content. But they that will be rich fall into temptation and a snare, and into many foolish and hurtful lusts, which drown men in destruction and perdition. For the love of money is the root of all evil: which while some coveted after, they have erred from the faith, and pierced themselves through with many sorrows. But thou, O man of God, flee these things; and follow after righteousness, godliness, faith, love, patience, meekness."

Your goal in life is not to break your neck to get that job or better grade, or that husband or wife......

Do not get me wrong, you are to motivate yourself to do better in life, but what I am saying is, you are to put God first in all that you do in life and watch everything else follow. Do you know your identity in Chris? The saints are heirs through Christ.

ST. Matthew 6:30-34 "Wherefore, if God so clothe the grass of the field, which today is, and tomorrow is cast into the oven, shall he not much more clothe you, O ye of little faith? Therefore, take no thought, saying, what shall we eat: or what shall we drink? Or Wherewithal shall we be clothed?

(For after all these things do the Gentiles seek) for your heavenly Father knoweth that ye have need of all these things. But seek ye first the kingdom of God, and his righteousness; and all these. Things shall be added unto you. Take therefore no thought for the morrow: for the morrow shall take thought for the things of itself. Sufficient unto the day is the evil thereof."

Obeying God's Word, and keeping his statues, paying your tithes (10% of your first increase) and giving from a pure heart (man's heart = man's spirit) is what he expects of us. You cannot pick and choose which commandments you will obey in his Word and which ones you will ignore. You must love God with all your heart, body, and soul (soul = mind, will, emotions). Naked came you into this world, and naked shall you leave out. Set your heart on the things of God.

JESUS is Lord.!!!

Jesus Is Lord

Did you know that JESUS is LORD??

There is no other God, and that the Holy Ghost is God's spirit. NO ONE ELSE! I am in a personal relationship with an alive Jesus Christ, who has been ordained by God to take away the sins of the world, who is soon to come back. There is no one else that has been ordained by God to take away yours sins, not buddha, not mohammed, or any other false god. You cannot be saved but by one way and that is through Jesus Christ. He is your way in, he is your way out. Anyone who do not believe this is under spiritual attack by an antichrist demon.
ST. JOHN 3:13-21, "And no man hath ascended up to heaven, but he that came down from heaven, even the Son of man which is in heaven. And as Moses lifted up the serpent in the wilderness, even so must the Son of man be lifted up: That whosoever believeth in him should not perish but have eternal life. For God so loved the world, that he gave his only begotten Son, that whosoever believeth in him should not perish, but have everlasting life. For God sent not his Son into the world to condemn the world; but that the world through him might be saved. He that believeth on him is not condemned: but he that believeth not is condemned already, because he hath not believed in the name of the only begotten Son of God. And this is the condemnation, that light is come into the world, and men loved darkness rather than light, because their deeds were evil. For everyone that doeth evil hateth the light, neither cometh to the light, lest his deeds should be reproved. But he that doeth

truth cometh to the light, that his deeds may be made manifest, that they are wrought in God."
ROMANS 10:9-10, "That is thou shalt confess with thy mouth the Lord Jesus, and shalt believe in thin heart that God hath raised him from the dead, thou shalt be saved. For with the heart man believeth unto righteousness; and with the mouth confession is made unto salvation."
PHILIPPIANS 2:8-11, "And being found in fashion as a man, he humbled himself, and became obedient unto death, even the death of the cross. Wherefore God also hath highly exalted him and given him a name which is above every name. That at the name of Jesus every knee should bow, of things in heaven, and things in earth, and things under the earth; And that every tongue should confess that Jesus Christ is Lord, to the glory of God the Father."
ROMANS 13:1-2, "Let every soul be subjet unto the higher powers. For ther is no power but of God: the powers that be are ordained of God. Whosoever therefore resisteth the power, resisteth the ordinance of God: and they that resist shall receive to themselves damnation."
ROMANS 14:7-9, "For none of us liveth to himself, and no man dieth to himself. For whether we live, we live unto the Lord: and whether we die, we die unto the Lord, whether we live therefore, or die, we are the Lord's. For to this end Christ both died, and rose, and revived, that he might be Lord both of the dead and living."

STOP BEING DECEIVED......JESUS IS LORD AND THERE IS NO OTHER. HEAVEN AND HELL IS REAL, WHILE WE STILL GOT TIME, GET YOUR LIFE IN ORDER WITH GOD, BEFORE HE RETURN. REPENT (STOP AND TURN, STOP SINNING AND TURN FROM YOUR WICKED WAYS, ASK GOD FOR FORGIVNESS (1 JOHN 1:8-9), ACCEPT JESUS AS YOUR LORD AND

SAVIOR) AND BE BAPTIZED IN THE NAME OF JESUS CHRIST AND YE SHALL RECEIVE THE GIFT OF THE HOLY GHOST (GOD'S SPIRIT) ACTS 2:38

The Holy Ghost

I JOHN 5:7, "For there are three that bear record in heaven, the Father, the Word, and the Holy Ghost: and these three are one" ST. JOHN 1:1 "In the beginning was the Word, and the Word was with God, and the Word was God."

Yes, God is the Father, and Jesus is the only begotten son of God, they are one, because God is in Jesus and Jesus is in God. The Word (which is Jesus) came down in the form of flesh and dwelt among us. See, there is nothing that you are going through that God cannot relate to. His Word tells us that his own turned their backs on him. Jesus came that we might have life and have it more abundantly.

ST. JOHN 10:10 "The thief (the devil) cometh not, but for to steal, and to kill, and to destroy I am come that they might have life, and that they might have it more abundantly."

PHILIPPIANS 2:10-11, "That at the name of Jesus every knee should bow, of things in heaven, and things in the earth, and things under the earth; and that every tongue should confess that Jesus Christ is Lord, to the glory of God the Father."

ST. JOHN 1:1-5, "In the beginning was the Word, and the Word was with God, and the Word was God. The same was in the beginning with God. All things were made by him; and without him was not anything made that was made. In him was life; and the life was the light of men. And the light shineth in darkness; and the darkness comprehended it not."

DEUTERONOMY 4:39 "Know therefore this day, and consider it in thine heart, that the Lord he is God in heaven above and upon the earth beneath: there is no one else."

Praise the Lord everyone!!! This message is about the **HOLY GHOST** (which is God's spirit) ….

Did you know that just going to church (Apostolic/Pentecostal church that baptizes in the Name of Jesus and teaches about the gift of the HOLY GHOST- which is God's spirit.) is not enough???

You must be taught about the gift of the Holy Ghost.

(King James Bible) ACTS chapter 2 verses 38-39, "Then Peter said unto them, Repent, and be baptized every one of you in the name of Jesus Christ for the remission of sins, and ye shall receive the gift of the Holy Ghost. For the promise is unto you, and to your children, and to all that are afar off, even as many as the Lord our God shall call."

ST. JOHN chapter 3 verses 1-5, "There was a man of the Pharisees, named Nicodemus, a ruler of the Jews: The same came to Jesus by night, and said unto him, Rabbi, we know that thou art a teacher come from God: for no man can do these miracles that thou doest, except God be with him. Jesus answered and said unto him, Verily, verily, I say unto thee, except a man be born again, he cannot see the kingdom of God. Nicodemus saith unto him, how can a man be born when he is old? Can he enter the second time into his mother's womb, and be born? Jesus answered, Verily, verily, I say unto thee, except a man be born of water and of the Spirit, he cannot enter into the kingdom of God."

What it means to be saved/born again, is

1st accepting the Lord Jesus as your Lord and Savior.

(believing in your heart that Jesus is the son of God and they are one. Yes JESUS IS GOD.- 1John 5:7, "For there are three that bear record in heaven, the Father, the Word, and the Holy Ghost: and these three are one" –also PHILIPPIANS 2:9-11, "Wherefore God also hath highly exalted him, and given him a name which is above every name: That at the name of Jesus every knee should bow, of things in heaven, and things in earth, and things under the earth; And that every tongue should confess that Jesus Christ is Lord, to the glory of God the Father.")

2nd repenting from your sins (which means asking for forgiveness of all your sins from God and to stop committing them and turning from them.)

3rd being baptized in the Name of Jesus,

4th then tarrying for the Holy Ghost (which means receiving God's spirit in you and speaking in other tongues as the Spirit of God gives you utterance) THE <u>HOLY GHOST</u>:

ST. JOHN 14:26, "But the Comforter, which is the Holy Ghost, whom the Father will send in my name, he shall teach you all things, and bring all things to your remembrance whatsoever I have said unto you."

ST. JOHN 15:26, "But when the Comforter is come, whom I will send unto you from the Father, even the Spirit of truth, which proceedeth from the Father, he shall testify of me:"

ST. JOHN 16:13-15, "Howbeit when he, the Spirit of truth, is come, he will guide you into all truth: for he shall not speak of himself; but whatsoever he shall hear, that shall he speak, and he will shew you things to come. He shall glorify me: for he shall receive of mine and shall shew it unto you. All things that the Father hath are mine: therefore, said I, that he shall take of mine, and shall shew it unto you."

ACTS 2:1-4, "And when the day of Pentecost was fully come, they were all with one accord in one place. And suddenly there came a sound from heaven as of a rushing mighty wind, and it filled all the house where they were sitting. And there appeared unto them cloven tongues like as of fire, and it sat upon each of them. And they were all filled with the Holy Ghost, and began to speak with other tongues, as the Spirit gave them utterance."

1 CORINTHIANS 2:11-14, "For what man knoweth the things of a man, save the spirit of man which is in him? Even so the things of God knoweth no man, but the Spirit of God. Now we have received, not the spirit of the world, but the spirit which is of God; that we might know the things that are freely given to us of God. Which things also we speak, not in the words which man's wisdom teacheth, but which the Holy Ghost teacheth, comparing spiritual things with spiritual. But the natural man receiveth not the things of the Spirit of God: for they are foolishness unto him: neither can he know them, because they are spiritually discerned."

So, we learn here that the HOLY GHOST is a comforter. You mean to tell me, that whenever I am feeling down or sad or even mad, the HOLY GHOST will comfort me, because that is the Holy Ghost's job? YES ☺!!!! Ok next, the HOLY GHOST will guide me into all truth, and show me things to come. WOW!!! The Holy Ghost is a helper.... So, when you need help in any area in your life the Holy Ghost is there (granted you are saved and filled with God's Holy Spirit) to help you and bring all things to your remembrance. WOW what an awesome gift from God...... ☺ ISN'T IT A BEAUTIFUL THING TO LIVE FOR THE LORD JESUS?

Be Not Deceived

Praise the Lord everyone! Be not **DECEIVIED**. Did you know that going to church (Apostolic/Pentecostal church that baptizes in the Name of Jesus and teaches about the gift of the HOLY GHOST-which is God's spirit.) and just hearing the Word of God being preached is not enough????

Well, it seems that some people go to church just to say they went to church, and when you ask them well, what did the pastor preach on, or they tell you however, when you ask them what you understood about it......they have no answer. Or some are under the deception that as long as they attend church that they are living right or for the Lord. This friend is a huge DECEPTION...

In the King James Bible, James chapter 1 verse 22 says, "But be ye doers of the word, and not hearers only, deceiving your own selves."

We are to hear the word of God and obey the word of God my friend ☺! Yes, this means obeying EVERYTHING God says for us to do and not to do, in his Word. We are not to pick and choose what we will obey, but we are to obey all of God's Word.

Otherwise, how could you see God's glory (which is manifested goodness) in your life? How could you receive the blessings of the Lord, if you are disobeying his word because God does not reward evil (which is anything that goes against the Word of God)?

In the King James Bible, Deuteronomy chapter 28 verse 1-2 says,

"And it shall come to pass, if thou shalt hearken diligently unto the voice of the Lord thy God, to observe and to do all his commandments which I command thee this day, that the Lord thy God will set thee on high above all nations of the earth: And all these blessings shall come on thee, and overtake thee, if thou shalt hearken unto the voice of the Lord thy God."

So, my friend, we as saints of God must be hearers and doers of God's Word, otherwise how would you be able to tell/see the difference between the saved (saints of God) and the unsaved (those that go against God's word/disobey God's word/serving sin rather than God)?????

JESUS is Lord!!!! Jesus loves you more than you know…

In His Presence

Do you really know what we (as saints) get when we dwell in the secret place **(presence) of the highest God**??????

Psalms 91:1-3, "He that dwelleth in the secret place of the most high shall abide under the shadow of the almighty. I will say of the Lord, He is my refuge and my fortress: my God, in him will I trust. Surely, he shall deliver thee from the snare of the fowler, and from the noisome pestilence."

Psalms 31:20, "Thou shalt hide them in the secret of thy presence from the pride of man: (So pride means conceited, self-respect, or haughtiness (proud)). thou shalt keep them secretly in a pavilion (Pavilion means light roofed structure for shelter or housing) from the strife of tongues." (Strife means heated, often violent dissension, bitter conflict (difference of opinion, battle, or war) struggle, fight, or competition between rivals)

Psalms 27:5, "For in the time of trouble he shall hide me in his pavilion: (So, in the time of trouble we are hidden in his pavilion (a light roofed structure for shelter) in the secret of his tabernacle shall he hide me; he shall set me up upon a rock." (Now the tabernacle (the portable sanctuary in which Israel carried the Ark of the Covenant through the desert, when God delivered them out of Egypt-Exodus chapters 24-31) represents heaven, Hebrews 9:11, so we see that this is all speaking of the presence of the Lord or his secret place.)

Psalms 91:1, "He that dwelleth in the secret place of the most high shall abide under the shadow of the almighty." Ref:

Psalms 91:2, "I will say of the Lord, He is my refuge and my fortress: my
God: in him will I trust."

(Refuge means protection, shelter, a source of help, relief, or comfort) (Fortress means- A fortified (to make strong, to reinforce, by adding materials to give emotional, moral, or mental strength to) place.)

> Psalms 18:2, "The Lord is my rock, and my fortress, and my deliverer; my God, my strength, in whom I will trust; my buckler, and the horn of my salvation, and my high tower."

We see here that God is your rock, strength, deliverer.... BUCKLER- Psalms 91:4, "He shall cover thee with his feathers, and under his wings shalt thou trust: his truth (his Word/his Spirit) shall be thy shield and buckler."

Isaiah 55:11, "So shall my word be that goeth forth out of my mouth: it shall not return unto me void, but it shall accomplish that which I please, and it shall prosper in the thing whereto I sent it."

God's word (which is God, ST. John 1:1," In the beginning was the Word, and the Word was with God, and the Word was God.") will not return unto him void. God is your buckler because he is truth. According to his word, his truth shall be thy shield (protection) and buckler (PSALMS 91:4). Why??? Because his word cannot return unto him void. So, because his word must obey God, WHEN YOU SPEAK HIS WORD, it shall come to pass.

> Psalms 91:3, "Surely he shall deliver thee from the snare of the fowler, and from the noisome pestilence."

God delivers you from the snare (trapping device, something that serves to entangle the unwary) of the fowler and from the noisome pestilence (this is talking about principalities, powers, rulers of the darkness of this world, and spiritual wickedness Ephesians 6:11-13)

So again, these scriptures represent what we (saints) have when we dwell in the secret place of the most high God. Remember, when speaking God's word, you must first believe that he is able to do just what he said he will do. So, find a scripture in the bible that relates to what you are going through and speak that scripture over your circumstances 24/7, all while believing that what you speak shall and has already come to pass (that is called walking by faith). ☺

How you dwell in the secret place of the most High God is by being willingly and obedient to his word. This is constantly making sure that your <u>lifestyle</u> is according to the Word of the Lord. Whatever does not line up with the Word of God, is not of God. So, it is very important not to let the cares and riches of this world choke the seed (God's Word) that is in you. Please keep in mind that worry is not of God, and panic is groundless fear…… We must continue to sow our much-needed seed which is God's Word in our heart. Remember, how much you sow is how much you shall reap…….so, if you sow little Word in your heart and life, then you will reap little. No Word, no faith, little Word, little faith

<u>Much Word, much faith</u> ☺

So, sow the much-needed seed in your heart and water that seed with your faith daily. Walk by faith, find your scripture, and post it on your mirror, speak your scripture daily 24/7, keep your eyes on our Lord Jesus Christ, don't look to the left or the right, just stay meditating and running references in God's Word day and night. If you draw closer to God, he will draw closer to you, and remember for his Word which is God, cannot lie!

JESUS is Lord!!!! Jesus loves you more than you know............

Man's True Identity

1 Thessalonians 5:23, "And the very God of peace sanctify you wholly; and I pray God your whole spirit and soul and body be preserved blameless unto the coming of our Lord Jesus Christ."

Man is a Spirit, who possesses a Soul (mind, will, emotions, personality, and countenance) and lives in a physical Body.

You do not have a spirit; you are a spirit. Your body does not possess a soul; your body has a brain.

(King James Bible) Genesis 1:26-27, "And God said, let us make man in our image after our likeness: and let them have dominion over the fish of the sea, and over the fowl of the air, and over the cattle, and over all the earth, and over every creeping thing that creepeth upon the earth. So, God created man in his own image, in the image of God created he him; male and female created he them." Genesis 2:7, "And the Lord God formed man of the dust of the ground and breathed into his nostrils the breath of life; and man became a living soul." ST. John 4:24, "God is a Spirit: and they that worship him must worship him in spirit and in truth."

The part of you that looks like God, which is the real you, is the Spirit man. The spirit man is the core of your being, it is what gives you life, it's what causes your soul to live, and your body to live. You do not have a spirit; you are a <u>spirit.</u> You live in a house called the Body, but you are a spirit. You live in the house of a physical body so that you can have comprehension and be able to have authority over physical things. You are a spirit made in the image of God, you possess a soul, and you live in a physical body.

You cannot contact your spirit through your emotions or your physical body.

The spirit realm cannot be naturally seen or felt. (we live in a physical realm and running concurrently or at the same time that this physical world is running, there is a spiritual world running at the same time.)

However, in the natural you cannot in the natural, see or feel that spiritual world. (King James Bible) 2 Corinthians 5:6, "Therefore we are always confident, knowing that, whilst we are at home in the body, we are absent from the Lord."

So, while I'm here in my body, and you're here in your body, we are not with the Lord, we are not in the realm of the spirit; we are in this physical world.

So the spirit realm cannot be naturally seen or felt, so while I can touch your body (my hand touch your arm), I can touch your soul with words (you can feel that, I can say words to make you feel good, or say words to make you feel sad, or words that make you angry or words that hurt you, your Soul can be touched in this physical realm), but you cannot touch your spirit, or see or touch the spiritual realm while you are in this physical body, unless God opens your eyes up, like he did a few people in the bible.

The only way to perceive spiritual truth then, is through the Word of God. (King James Bible) ST John 6:63," It is the spirit that quickeneth; the flesh profiteth nothing: the words that I speak unto you, they are spirit, and they are life." So, the Word of God is the only way to perceive (to become aware of, to know, to recognize, understand) spiritual truth.

The Word of God is what makes us aware of spiritual things. So, it is only by our belief and faith in the Word of God, that we have any understanding in the spiritual realm. Subtract the Word of God from this equation, and we are stuck in a physical, natural, carnal, understanding with no contact to spiritual things.

The Word of God is the key to the successful operation that we have in life.

James 1:23-25, "For if any be a hearer of the word, and not a doer, he is like unto a man beholding his natural face in a glass: For he beholdeth himself, and goeth his way, and straightway forgetteth what manner of man he was. But whoso looketh into the perfect law of liberty, and continueth therein, he being not a forgetful hearer, but a doer of the work,

this man shall be blessed in his deed."

Just like you go into your bathroom, or bedroom, and you look into a mirror, and you behold a reflection of your natural body, now you have never looked directly at your natural body, that's a reflection in the mirror that is not you. Your eyes have never popped out and turned around and looked at you, straight at your body.

So, you have never seen, looked at your body, accept what you can see with your eyes (still in your head), looking at other parts of your body (arms, hands, foot, legs etc....), but you have never looked eyeball to eyeball at your body. What you see in the mirror is a reflection, I know it is not the real you, because that reflection cannot be touched. It is just a reflection, but you have grown to trust that reflection, the reflection shows you that a hair is out of place, and you trust it enough to put the hair in place.

Well so the bible likens this thing, like that mirror will show you a reflection of your naturally, physical body, so the bible is like a mirror, it's like a glass, that when you look in the bible, it will show you a true reflection of your spirit.

NOTE: When you get born again, your spirit man has changed completely. So, you want to know what my spirit man looks like now, well, when you look in the bible, you are looking at a reflection of your spirit man.

When you got born again, the part of you that got born again was your spirit. Your spirit man was completely and totally changed, it was made perfect, it was made mature, it was completely and totally changed exactly like <u>Jesus</u> and not your soul or your body, but your spirit was. So, if you want to know what your spirit man looks like after you got born again, open the bible up and that's exactly how you look like.

You keep looking at your performance in your soul and your body (not living a perfect life, or didn't do that right), the bible is a reflection of the perfect part of you which is your spirit. One third of you is perfect; one third of you is just like God. That part of you, the day you got saved, and your spirit became perfect, flawless, mature, and that is the part that looks just like God the day you got saved.

2 Corinthians 5:17-18, "Therefore if any man be in Christ, he is a new creature: old things are passed away; behold, all things are become new. And all things are of God, who hath reconciled us to himself by Jesus Christ, and hath given to us the ministry of reconciliation; "

God is making reference to your born-again spirit. So, every born-again believer has gone through a complete inner transformation. Which means, your spirit man right now is as perfect, mature, and complete as Jesus himself. Now that you are born again, you are not in the process of trying to get anything from God; everything you will ever need in the Christian life is already present in its entirety, in YOUR SPIRIT.

The day you got born again, you and God, you and the Holy Ghost (which is God's spirit) were married. Now that you got born again, the spirit of God moved in your spirit, so you and the spirit of God are one. When God became one with your spirit, he released everything in HIM…. in you.

So, you are trying to get something from him, but everything of him, he has already given to you. So, it's not a matter of trying to get something from him, it's a matter of recognizing what you already got!!!!!!!

You in bondage, lack, sick and asking God to help you, and he says I already gave it to you; you just need to know how to access it……continue.

NOTE: You trying to perceive this with your soul and with your body, and the only way to perceive what is being said is through the Word of God and your faith in the Word of God. (King James Bible) Ephesians 3:16," That he would grant you, according to the riches of his glory, to be strengthened with might by his Spirit in the inner man; "

Might is the ability to do anything. You have been strengthened with might, by the Holy Ghost. So, you right now have the power, (Ephesians 1:18-20 that raised Jesus from the dead), has been deposited in your spirit, you have the abilities, everything that Jesus had when he was on the earth (when the Word became flesh and dwelt among us ST. John 1:12-16), you have.

So, we who are born again have already received the fullness of his power, the fullness of his anointing. You just have to know how to access it.

(SAINTS/BORN AGAIN BELIEVERS) You have healing in you right now, you have deliverance, wisdom, and the spirit of might in you right now, you have the power to raise the dead in you right now, you just don't know how to access it. •So, if you do not know how to access it, you can die of sickness, walking around full of healing, because you had no way in your body or your soul to perceive that healing existed accept through the word and some would not believe the Word, they only believed what they could feel and what their soul told them. So, if they could not perceive it with the natural means, and they did not believe the Word, then they were subject to the natural issue and they died and right there in the makeup was all of the healing they ever needed but they could not access it. It is not about trying to get something from God once you are born again, the only two things you need to do for the rest of your life is RENEW YOUR MIND (Joshua 1:8, Romans 12:1-2) AND RELEASE......

So, you have a soul, and you live in a natural body, you cannot contact the spirit through natural means. And you cannot receive from the spirit, trying to contact him (your spirit) through natural means.

The spirit believes the word. Flesh things go with flesh things and spiritual things go with spiritual things, but Jesus said the words that I speak unto you is spirit.

So if my spirit believes the Word (God's Word), and my soul believes the Word, then when your spirit and soul agree together, then when those two agree together (because the only way for your soul to perceive that the spirit is real is for your soul to believe the Word, your soul MUST take the Word, that he cannot see, feel, or touch, and just believe the Word, then your soul immediately hooks up with your spirit.) so then when your body is hurting, diagnosed with sickness, seeing how the spirit got healing and your soul agree with him (your spirit that agrees with the Word), you now have access to that healing that the spirit has, that can now be released through your soul to your body!!!!!

So, everything your spirit has only requires your soul to agree with in order for your body to have it.

The body believes the five senses, what he can taste, touch, smell, feel, and see, meanwhile, the spirit believes the Word of GOD, then when pain comes on the body and tell the body this hurts, the soul has to have been renewing its mind in the Word of God day and night, so that the soul can say, no I do not agree to the body, cause I believe the Word, and the Word says we are healed (Isaiah 53:5) and now what has happened is, by the soul teaming up with the spirit and believing the Word of God, the soul now has access to the healing that the spirit possesses. It is the same thing dealing with marriages being in bondage, lack, poverty, stress, pressure, anger, hurt.... etc.

Decide that you will believe the Word of God all the time. You can go on a fast to let the body know that the soul and spirit does not follow the body. You fast to bring your body into subjection to the Word of God.

When your soul believes the body(senses) you get cut off from the spirit, but when you believe the Word of God along with the spirit, then you get access to everything that the spirit possesses. Renew your mind in the Word of God, renew, renew, renew, renew, renew. (King James Bible) Romans 8:6, "For to be carnally minded is death; but to be spiritually minded is life and peace."

When God says something is wrong, and it is wrong to do that, he is not trying to be pies, he's trying to say, if this is wrong, and you do this thing and it's wrong, it's going to tare something up.

Carnal mindedness equal death---sickness, discouragement, depression, loneness, lack, disease— this comes as a result of a carnal mind set. Carnality produces death and all of those things happen because your separated from God, it's a mindset that separates you from God which ultimately brings you to the cycle of death.

All sin is carnal, but all carnality is not sin. Meaning carnal (that of the five senses-see, touch, taste, smell, feel), carnality is what you hear, touch, taste, smell. Carnal mindedness is allowing your mind to be dominated by what you can see, hear, taste, smell and feel. You are carnal minded when your thoughts center primary on the physical realm. When your mind is dominated by your five senses, you are now in agreement by what your body believes, and you have been cut yourself off from the resources that have been deposited in your born-again spirit.

You are more than body and soul.

You must be in the Word meditating/studying day and night. Spiritual mindedness is that spiritual mind that releases the flow of God's life in you, but that carnal mind shuts its off………continue…

Acknowledge that you have healing, abundance, or whatever you need, acknowledge and agree, whatever it is through the Word of God, out of your mouth and BELIEVE, and because of that acknowledgement the faith of your releases it to the natural.

Philemon 1:6," That the communication of thy faith may become effectual by te acknowledging of every good thing which is in you in Christ Jesus."

Isaiah 26:3," Thou wilt keep him in perfect peace, whose mind is stayed on thee: because he trusteth in thee."

You cannot get peace when your mind is stayed on the problem. As your mind stays on God, your soul agrees with your spirit, and God's peace is released into your soul and your body.

Peace, which is an emotion, is linked to the way you think. Your lack of peace is not because of any circumstance or any person, your lack of peace is because you have allowed your mind to be dominated by what you can see, hear, taste, touch and feel. Your busy thinking about the potential damage, but all a while God's peace has been present in your spirit, but you haven't drawn it out, you have kept the vial closed and you're saying I don't have any peace because of that problem, or person, or circumstance, no, you don't have peace because you got your mind on that. Worrying is a sin because it is an attachment to the carnal mind.

You ought to be meditating on what the Word says. It's all about where you are putting your soul. Keeping your mind on what the Word says will keep your in total peace. Do not rent space in your mind to somebody. I cannot trust man, but I can trust God and it is taken care of.

Believers should not live like lost people who are trapped in their carnal physical world. (King James Bible) Ephesians 4:17-27," This I say therefore, and testify in the Lord, that ye henceforth walk not as other Gentiles walk, in the vanity of their mind, Having the understanding darkened, being alienated from the life of God through the ignorance that is in them, because of the blindness of their heart: Who being past feeling have given themselves over unto lasciviousness, to work all uncleanness with greediness. But ye have not so learned Christ; If so, be that ye have heard him, and have been taught by him, as the truth is in Jesus: That ye put off concerning the former conversation the old man, which is corrupt according to the deceitful lusts; And be renewed in the spirit of your mind; And that ye put on the new man, which after God is created in righteousness and true holiness. Wherefore putting away lying, speak every man truth with his neighbor: for we are members one of another. Be ye angry, and sin not: let not the sun go down upon your wrath: Neither give place to the devil." The knowledge of God is absolutely critical but must be understood in order to be useful.

Without understanding you can't release the life that's in your spirit without understanding. Do not have religious illusion of God and us and how stuff works, but UNDERSTAND God's Word so you can know how to skillfully use his Word in your life and intelligently live the life and gain what needs to be gained. JESUS is Lord!!!! Jesus loves you more than you know.

The Tongue

THE TONGUE… Oh What DYNAMITE!!

Huh?? What do you mean words are just words, what's wrong with just talking???? Did you know that words can destroy people? Yes, the tongue has the power of life and death. Even truthful words can damage and yet can also save a friend from going the wrong way.

PROVERBS 15:4, "A wholesome tongue is a tree of life: but perverseness therein is a breach in the spirit."

This means that the tongue that brings healing is a tree of life, but a deceitful tongue crushes the spirit.

PROVERBS 18:21, "Death and life are in the power of the tongue: and they that love it shall eat the fruit thereof." ST MATTHEW 12:36-37, "But I say unto you, that every idle word that men shall speak, they shall give account thereof in the day of judgment. For by thy words thou shalt be justified, and by thy words thou shalt be condemned." PROVERBS 12:18, "There is that speaketh like the piercings of a sword: but the tongue of the wise is health." PROVERBS 13:3, "He that keepeth his mouth keepeth his life: but he that openeth wide his lips shall have destruction." This means that he who guards his lips guards his life, but he who speaks rashly will come to ruin.

PROVERBS 16:23-24, "The heart of the wise teacheth his mouth, and addeth learning to his lips. Pleasant words are as a honeycomb, sweet to the soul,
and health to the bones."

JAMES 3:2, "For in many things we offend all, if any man offend not in word, the same is a perfect man, and able also to bridle the whole body." JAMES 3:5, 6, 8, 10, "Even so the tongue is a little member, and boasteth great things. Behold, how great a matter a little fire kindleth!

Ref: PROVERBS 26:20, "Where no wood is, there the fire goeth out: so, where there is no talebearer, the strife ceaseth." V:6) And the tongue is a fire, a world of iniquity so is the tongue among our members, that it defileth the whole body, and setteth on fire the course of nature, and it is set on fire of hell. Ref: ST MATTHEW 15:11, "Not that which goeth into the mouth defileth a man; but that which cometh out of the mouth, this defileth a man." V:8) But the tongue can no man tame; it is an unruly evil, full of deadly poison. Ref: PSALMS 140:3, "They have sharpened their tongues like a serpent; adders' poison is under their lips. Selah" V:10) Out of the same mouth proceedeth blessing and cursing. My brethren, these things ought not so to be."

Proverbs 15:1," A soft answer turneth away wrath: but grievous words stir up anger." PROVERBS 21:23, "Whoso keepeth his mouth and his tongue keepeth his soul from troubles." PSALMS 45:1, "My heart is inditting a good matter: I speak of the things which I have made touching the king: my tongue is the pen of a ready writer."

WOW, so as you can see, people are not even aware of exactly what comes out of their mouth.

WHEN YOU SAY, YOU SOW....

Either you are going to sow life (health, prosperity, wisdom, might, joy), or you are going to sow death (depression, anger, sickness, jealousy, strife (bitter conflict, contention, fight), fear, discouragement).

Stop putting your eyes on your circumstances because when you do that you begin to speak negatively. Put your eyes on the Word of God and stand still and see the salvation of the Lord. (II CHRONICLES 20:1-18)

Here is something else to put on your mind....

When you say, you sow and what you reap is what you are more developed in, either you will reap fear or faith.

So, watching what you say is essential, not just about ourselves but also what we say to/about others. When our Lord and Savior Jesus Christ returns, we all will be judged on our words that came forth out of our mouth.

So, you ask the question, well how am I speaking negatively upon myself?

I'm glad you asked, when your body feels pain, you say "oh I'm sick", so then you are sick however, when someone who has been sowing the Word of God (which is your seed) in their heart (your spirit-which is the ground you sow in) day and night (meditating- JOSHUA 1:8) and they feel pain upon their body, guess what they reap.......they reap the thing that they are more developed in, which is faith in the Word of God. They show that they trust God by resting in him. Let me tell you what I mean, they 1st believe the Word of God,

2nd they find their healing scriptures (ISAIAH 53:5, I PETER 2:24, JAMES 5:16), 3rd they meditate on those scriptures, 4th they speak by faith healing over their body, 5th they reap healing!!!!(standing still and seeing the salvation of the Lord) ☺

And the same goes for issues concerning lack (PHILIPPIANS 4:19, PSALMS 23:1&6, ST LUKE 6:38, DEUTERONOMY 28:1-2, &8), a husband (must first understand why you were created, marriage, divorce, and the position of an husband (head of the household), wife(helpmate), and they two shall become one, GENESIS chapters 2 & 3, I CORITHIANS 7:1-40, ST MATTHEW 5:31-32, EPHESIANS 5:28-33) a wife), a job, a car, wisdom (JAMES 1:5-8), strength.

(II CORINTHIANS 12:9, PHILIPPIANS 4:19)

Try it!!!!! Start speaking positively over your life, and when someone does wrong to you (yeah, I'm talking about you people with road rage, women mad at men, men mad at women, students mad at teachers, parents' word-of-mouthing their children to their friends, employees on their jobs, church folk to one another), instead of you bad mouthing them, try just keeping your mouth closed. Instead thank God the situation was not worser than it was.

Remember to keep a humble mind-set and to be of a meek and quiet spirit. Be led by God and not your feelings or words....

JESUS is Lord!!!! Jesus loves you more than you know.

Don't Believe the Lie

STOP STOP!!!!
A lie has been told to deceive the whole world…Do you know **where the first man and woman came from** and why you were created???????

Genesis 1:26-30, "And God said, let us make man in our image, after our likeness: and let them have dominion over the fish of the sea, and over the fowl of the air, and over the cattle, and over all the earth, and over every creeping thing that creepeth upon the earth. So, God created man in his own image, in the image of God created he him: male and female created he them. And God blessed them, and God said unto them, be fruitful, and multiply, and replenish the earth, and subdue it: and have dominion over the fish of the sea, and over the fowl of the air, and over every living thing that moveth upon the earth. And God said, Behold, I have given you every herb bearing seed, which is upon the face of all the earth, and every tree, in the which is the fruit of a tree yielding seed; to you it shall be for meat. And to every beast of the earth, and to every fowl of the air, and to everything that creepeth upon the earth, wherein there is life, I have given every green herb for meat: and it was so."

Man was created in God's image after his likeness. Now remember man is a spirit, that possesses a soul (which is your will, emotions, personality, mind), and lives in a physical body (which is flesh). So, when the bible speaks on man is created in God's image, it is speaking on man's spirit being created in the image of God, remember, God is a spirit. Man had dominion (control) over fish, fowl of the air (birds), cattle (animals), all the earth, and all creeping things upon the earth (insects, spiders, etc...) God created man in his own image, creates male and female.

Male and female were created to be fruitful, multiply, and replenish (to fill and make complete again) the earth, also to subdue (to conquer) it (talking about earth). You were not created to fulfill your will but God's will.

Did you know that children are a gift from God?

Ref: Psalms 127:3, "Lo, children are a heritage of the Lord: and the fruit of the womb is his reward."

Genesis 33:5, "And he lifted up his eyes, and saw the women and the children; and said, who are those with thee? And he said, the children which God hath graciously given thy servant."

Now listen what God gives them (male and female), God gave them every herb bearing seed (now herbs are used for medicine or as seasoning for food).

Male and female had medicine and seasoning for food.

God gave them every tree with fruit yielding seed as food. So, we see here that God gave them trees that bear every kind of fruit there is. So male and female lacked for nothing, meaning, they had everything that they would need already.

There's an Answer for That

Genesis 2:1-25, "Thus the heavens and the earth were finished, and all the host of them. And on the seventh day God ended his work which he had made; and he rested on the seventh day from all his work which he had made. And God blessed the seventh day and sanctified it: because that in it he had rested from all his work which God created and made. These are the generations of the heavens and of the earth when they were created, I the day that the Lord God made the earth and the heavens, and every plant of the field before it was in the earth, and every her of the field before it grew: for the Lord God had not caused it to rain upon the earth, and there was not a man to till the ground. But there went up a mist form the earth and watered the whole face of the ground. And the Lord God formed man of the dust of the ground and breathed into his nostrils the breath of life; and man became a living soul. And the Lord God planted a garden eastward in Eden; and there he put the man whom he had formed. And out of the ground made the Lord God to grow every tree that is pleasant to the sight, and good for food, the tree of life also in the midst of the garden, and the tree of knowledge of good and evil. And a river went out of Eden to water the garden; and from thence it was parted and became into four heads. The name of the first is Pison: that is, it which compasseth the whole land of Havilah where there is good. And the good of that land is good; there is bdellium and the onyx stone. And the name of the second river is Gihon: the same is it that compasseth the whole land of Ethiopia. And the name of the third river is Hiddekel: that is, it which goeth toward the east of Assyria. And fourth river is Euphrates. And the Lord God took the man, saying, of every tree of the garden thou mayest freely eat: But of the tree of the knowledge of good and evil, thou shalt not eat of it; for in the day that thou eatest thereof thou shalt surely die. And the Lord God said, it is not good that the man should be alone; I will make him a help meet for him. And out of the ground the Lord God formed every beast of the field, and every fowl of the air; and brought them unto Adam to see what he would call them: and whatsoever Adam called every living creature, that was the name thereof. And Adam gave names to all cattle, and to the fowl of the air, and to every beast of the field; but for Adam there was not found a help meet for him. And the Lord God caused a deep sleep to fall upon Adam, and he slept: and he took one of his ribs and closed up the flesh instead thereof; And the rib, which the Lord God had taken from man, made he woman, and brought her unto the man. And Adam said, this is now bone of my bones, and flesh of my flesh: she shall be called Woman, because she was taken out of Man. Therefore, shall a man leave his father and his mother, and shall cleave unto his wife: and they shall be one flesh. And they were both naked, the man and his wife, and were not ashamed."

God rested on the seventh day and sanctified (purify, dedicated) it.

God forms man from the dust of the ground, breaths into his nostrils, and man became a living soul. Now let me explain this, remember in Genesis 1:26 when God made man in his image, keep in mind that God is a spirit, and man was made a spirit after the image of God. So, we see that man was made a spirit that possesses a soul (will, mind, emotions, and personality). Now when God formed man from the dust of the ground, this is when God formed flesh, (remember man is a spirit that possesses a soul and lives in a physical body), so man which is a spirit at this time (prior to God forming flesh from the dust), now once God formed flesh, the spirit of man can now have a place to live in, then God breaths (the breath of life) into man's nostrils and man became a living soul. So this is how man became a living soul, 1st God made man in his image, this is when man is made a spirit, 2nd God forms man (flesh) from the dust of the ground, this is the physical body being made, and 3rd God breaths into the nostrils of the physical body and man now becomes a living soul (this is when the spirit was put into the body and GOD breathed the breath of life into the nostrils of man.)

Next, we see that woman was formed from the rib of man. So, Eve (1st woman on earth) was formed from the Adam's (1st man on earth) rib. Again, this symbolizes the joining of man and woman becoming one when they marry, referencing back on Genesis 2:22-24.

Yes, referencing back to Genesis 1:27, woman was made in the image of God, that is woman was made a spirit because God is a spirit. Then in Genesis 2:22-24, flesh is made for woman (which is a spirit at this time) to dwell in. That is, flesh was made so the spirit can have a place to live in on this earth. Remember that physical things go with physical things and spiritual things go with spiritual things. Man and woman was a spirit, but in order for them to dwell on the earth that God created, they had to put on flesh. So do not believe the <u>deception</u> that man came from apes. Man did not come from apes, but the flesh (physical body) was formed from the dust of the ground.

God puts man in the garden that he had planted eastward in Eden.

So, God makes out of the ground to grow every tree, so you have trees that are good for food, the tree of life in the midst of the garden, and the tree of knowledge of good and evil.

Ref: Revelations 22:2, "In the mist of the street of it, and on either side of the river, was there the tree of life, which bare twelve manner of fruits, and yielded her fruit every month: and the leaves of the tree were for the healing of the nations." God puts man (Adam)

in the garden to dress it and to keep it (cultivates, grow, plow, tend to…etc.) God commands man (Adam) saying, he could eat of every tree, except of the tree of the knowledge of good and evil. God tells him, that in the day that thou eateth thereof thou shalt surely die, meaning dying spiritually meaning to be cut off from the provisions of God or separated from God. At that moment man was unaware of good and evil, or even the fact that they were naked. Man was present with the Lord, meaning that man was dwelling in the presence of the Lord or had the same mind-set of the Lord. This was because man was obeying God's every word. See, when you are in sin, you are absent from the Lord. To disobey his word is to be absent from God. To be carnally (worldly or have a mind-set that goes along with the world) minded is death (either spiritually-meaning to be cut off from God or separated from him or physically-meaning you die off the earth), and to be spiritually minded is life (meaning to be born again (saved and filled with God's Holy Spirit) and obeying God's word, having your continence clear of any guilt, dwelling in the house of God (which is his presence).)

This was a commandment (Commandment is an order given with authority, to direct with authority, give orders to) that God gave man (Adam).

God is saying, that if man disobey him, he shall surely die (Genesis 2:16-17).

Listen, it is extremely important to obey the God's word. It is a matter of life or death….

Literally. God makes man a help mate. God makes out of the ground every beast of the field, and fowl of the air, and brings them to Adam, to name them. Wow check out the authority God gave Adam, if you ever wanted to know where animals, birds, and insects…. etc. got their name from, it was Adam who named them.

Now, why was this done, because that is what man was created for. To be fruitful and multiply, replenish the earth and subdue (to conquer) it. (Ref: Genesis 1:28) God gave man dominion over the earth, beast of the field, and fowls of the air. God causes a deep sleep to fall upon Adam and takes one of his ribs, then the flesh.

God make from that rib, woman, and brought her unto the man. Adam calls her woman, because she was taken out of man. So, we see that Adam not only named the animals, birds, and beast but he named Woman as well.

Man leaves his father and mother, and cleave unto wife, and they two become one flesh, meaning the joining in marriage when male and female (not male and male or female and female because that is an abomination unto the Lord—Leviticus 20:13) become one unit. Woman was made for man. We are their help mate (a helper, companion, a spouse, a partner).

When a man marries a wife, him leaving his parents and cleaving unto his wife signifies from the beginning the woman being made from Adam's rib and being bone of his bones, and flesh of his flesh. That is why they shall be one flesh. The one flesh is representing the flesh of his flesh, when woman was made form man's rib. This is why man is the head of his household. The husband is the head of the household and the wife is the helper or partner to the husband. See the husband has to realize his position as the head of the house hold- meaning making sure that his household is in order-obeying the word of God, children are being trained up in the word of God, him and his wife are staying prayerful and fasting that satan tempt them not (I Corinthians 7:4-5), husbands loving their wife like they love themselves (Ephesians 5:2829, 1 Peter 3:7, I Corinthians 7:3) and the wife is to submit themselves unto their husbands (Ephesians 5:22). Genesis 3:1-24, "Now the serpent was more subtil than any beast of the field which the Lord God had made. And he said unto the woman, Yea, hath God said, Ye shall not eat of every tree of the garden? And the woman said unto the serpent, we may eat of the fruit of the trees of the garden: But of the fruit of the tree, which is in the midst of the garden, God hath said, Ye shall not eat of it, neither shall ye touch it, lest ye die. And the serpent said unto the woman, Ye shall not surely die: For God doth know that in the day ye eat thereof, then your eyes shall be opened, and ye shall be as gods, knowing good and evil. And when the woman saw that the tree was good for food, and that it was pleasant to the eyes, and a tree to be desired to make one wise, she took of the fruit thereof, and did eat, and gave also unto her husband with her; and he did eat. And the eyes of them both were opened, and they knew that they were naked; and they sewed fig leaves together and made themselves aprons And they heard the voice of the Lord God walking in the garden in the cool of the day: and Adam and his wife hid themselves from the presence of the Lord God amongst the trees of the garden. And the Lord God called unto Adam, and said unto him, Where art thou? And he said, I heard thy voice in the garden, and I was afraid, because I was naked: and I hid myself. And he said, who told thee that thou wast naked? Hast thou eaten of the tree, whereof I commanded thee that thou shouldest not eat? And the man said, the woman whom thou gavest to be with me, she gave me of the tree, and I did eat. And the Lord God said unto the woman, what is this that thou hast done? And the woman said, the serpent beguiled me, and I did eat. And the Lord God said unto the serpent, because thou hast done this, thou art cursed above all cattle, and above every beast of the field; upon thy belly shalt thou go, and dust shalt thou eat all the days of thy life: And I will put enmity between thee and the woman, and between thy seed and her seed; it shall bruise thy head, and thou shalt bruise his heel. Unto the woman he said, I will greatly multiply thy sorrow and thy conception; in sorrow thou shalt bring forth children; and thy desire shall be to thy husband, and he shall rule over thee. And unto Adam he said, Because thou hast hearkened unto the voice of thy wife, and hast eaten of the tree, of which I commanded thee, saying, Thou shalt not eat of it; cursed is the ground for thy sake; in sorrow shalt thou eat of it all the days of thy life; Thorns also and thistles shall it bring forth to thee; and thou shalt eat the herb of the field; In the sweat of thy face shalt thou eat bread, till thou return unto the ground; for out of it wast thou taken: for dust thou art, and unto dust shalt thou return. And Adam called his wife's name Eve, because she was the mother of all living. Unto Adam also and to his wife did the Lord

God make coats of skins and clothed them. And the Lord God said, Behold, the man is become as one of us, to know good and evil: and now, lest he put forth his hand, and take also of the tree of life, and eat, and live forever: Therefore, the Lord God sent him forth from the garden of Eden, to till the ground from whence he was taken. So, he drove out the man; and he placed at the east of the garden of Eden Cherubims, and a flaming sword which turned every way, to keep

the way of the tree of life."

The serpent (satan, devil) was more subtil (fine, delicate; subtle-clever, devious, crafty, operating in a hidden injurious way) than any beast of the field.

satan said unto the woman if God said unto her that she shall not eat of every tree of the garden.

NOTE: Now we see what satan is doing here, now God gave the commandment to the man (which is the head of the household). So, this commandment applies to the man and his household (the woman to), but because God did not say it to the woman, satan is trying to manipulate the woman into thinking that the commandment doesn't apply to her. But it did…...

The woman responds back to serpent by telling him what God said. They can eat of the fruit of the tree of the garden, except the fruit of the tree in the mist of the garden nor touch it lest ye die.

NOTE: Satan is trying the woman to see if she knows God's word that he hath spoken. It is important to know God's word and to obey it. Be totally sold out to God, because whatever curiosity you may have in you concerning anything outside the word of God, Satan will try you. That's why you need to pu7t on the Lord Jesus Christ and make not provision for the flesh to fulfill the lusts of thereof (Romans 13:14). Satan tells the woman she shall not die. NOTE: why is this said.... because Satan knows the woman does not know good and evil, and that she is spiritually present with the Lord. The woman may be thinking that she (if she disobeys God's word and eat of the tree in the mist of the garden) would die physically. Satan know that she would die spiritually because when we disobey God's word and sin, we are present with sin and absent from God.

Woman lust after tree, eats of the fruit of the tree in the mist of the garden, disobey God (even though the commandment was given unto Adam, Adam being the head of his household is to make sure his entire household obey God's word, when Eve disobeyed her husband, she ultimately disobeyed God, because the commandment came from God.), gave unto her husband and he (knowing God's commandment) disobeyed God.

1 John 2:16 talks about the lust of the flesh, the lust of the eyes, pride of life, is not of the Father, but is of the world……A lot of times we don't see or realize that God has given us all that we need. Man had dominion over all beast of the field, fowl of the air, and earth. Man and woman were created to be fruitful and multiply and replenish the earth and subdue (conquer) it (the earth). God gave them every herb yielding seed (again herbs are used for medicine and seasoning for food) and every tree with fruit yielding seed. So, they had food, medicine, seasoning for their food and was blessed of the Lord, given dominion over the earth, and you mean to tell me, they still wanted more??? So, having knowledge of good and evil was worth disobeying God's word and becoming spiritually absent from God????? I don't think so……... Here it is, man was in God's presence, man communed with God, why would you want to disobey God and risk losing his blessings? The bible teaches us to be content with such things as we have. They hear the voice of the Lord God walking in the garden and hide themselves from the presence of the Lord God.

God calls Adam .

Adam responds he heard him, hid himself because he was afraid and naked.

God questioned Adam who told him he was naked and did he disobey God's commandment. NOTES: Romans 3:5-12, talks about sin entered into the world, and death by sin, and so death passed upon all men…...Look what happened because of Adam's disobedience, death passed on all men why? Because the wages (payment) of sin is death. It is essential (extremely important) to obey God's word.

Adam blames woman for his disobedience.

Proverbs 28:13, "He that covereth his sins shall not prosper, but whoso confesseth and forsaketh them shall have mercy." 1 John 1:8-10, "If we say that we have no sin, we deceive ourselves, and the truth is not in us. If we confess our sins, he is faithful and just to forgive us our sins, and to cleanse us from all unrighteousness. If we say that we have not sinned, we make him a liar, and his word is not in us."

Take responsibility for your own actions, and repent (to stop and turn from your wicked ways) God questioned the woman. The woman blames the serpent

NOTES: 1 Timothy 2:14 talks about the woman being deceived was the transgression (Transgression is a sin committed against an individual, this is what Eve did when she disobeyed the head of her household, her husband's commandment that he got from God.)

Don't bring your members (the body/mind) under submission unto the devil. Don't even give ear to what he suggests. Stay steadfast in the word of God and trust/rest in God's word, which is God (ST. John 1:1-2).

This is a matter of life or death. Don't go against what God says in his word.

God curse satan above every beast of the field, pts him upon his belly, dust shalt he eats all the days of his life.

NOTES: There is chastisement (discipline) for disobeying God's word. God puts enmity (hatred) between the serpent and the woman.

God multiplies the woman's sorrow, in her sorrow she brings forth children, her desire is unto her husband, he shall rule over her. God curses the ground for Adam's sake, he shall eat of it all the days of his life.

Adam calls his wife's name Eve (meaning mother of all living).

The Lord God made coats of skins and clothed them.

God sent Adam forth from the garden of Eden.

NOTES: Because the serpent was cursed and made to eat dust all the days of his life, man was made from dust. So satan has a right to come after you, to attack you, because you were made from dust, and he is cursed to eat it all the days of his life. But OH, to be under the BLOOD OF JESUS. Just like in Egypt, when the spirit of death passed through the streets killing every first born of Egyptians but passed by the door post that had the blood on them (Exodus chapters 11 &12). When you are covered under the blood of Jesus, satan can't touch you. Obey God's word, stand on God's word, the devil is going to and from seeking whom he may devour, don't be caught uncovered. Stay in the presence of God 24/7. Don't cause a curse to come upon your house because of your disobedience to God's word.

WAKE UP!!!!!! 😬😬

the US House wants to make new rules and go gender neutral, He, she, father and mother, him, her, son, daughter — such terms may no longer be welcome in the upcoming 117th Congress if new changes to House rules are approved.

Wake up Christians!!!!

We must see the true agenda they are trying to push!!!

John 3:16, "For God so loved the world, that he gave his only begotten Son, that whosoever believeth in him should not perish, but have everlasting life." Look at the key words in this scripture, he, his, son, him....

They are trying to get rid of the bible!!! That is the ultimate agender and make room for the antichrist. They are trying to hide behind equality. You better know what you are voting for. God said his people parish because of lack of knowledge. Hosea 4:6, "My people are destroyed for lack of knowledge: because thou hast rejected knowledge, I will also reject thee, that thou shalt be no priest to me: seeing thou hast forgotten the law of thy God, I will also forget thy children."

The devil comes to steal, kill and destroy. Prayer worriers it is time now to pray in the Holy Ghost earnestly! Romans 12:2, "And be not conformed to this world: but be ye transformed by the renewing of your mind, that ye may prove what is that good, and acceptable, and perfect, will of God."

This is a crooked and perverse generation. Be not deceived. The world is calling what's wrong in God's eyes right. Do not I repeat do not conform to this world's way of thinking. We must renew our minds in the Word of God daily!! You will not know what God considers to be wrong or an abomination if you don't read...... 2 Timothy 2:1-7, "This know also, that in the last days perilous times shall come. For men shall be lovers of their own selves, covetous, boasters, proud, blasphemers, disobedient to parents, unthankful, unholy, without natural affection, trucebreakers, false accusers, incontinent, fierce, despisers of those that are good,

Traitors, heady, high-minded, lovers of pleasures more than lovers of God; Having a form of godliness but denying the power thereof: from such turn away. For of this sort are they which creep into houses, and lead captive silly women laden with sins, led away with divers' lusts,

Ever learning, and never able to come to the knowledge of the truth."

Homosexuality, lesbianism, transgender, bisexual is not of God. Stop being scare to tell the truth. Save them from going to hell. Hell is real, not everyone that dies is going to heaven. Tell the truth Christians, open your mouth and speak the Word BOLDLY!!!

Leviticus 18:22-23, "Thou shalt not lie with mankind, as with womankind: it is abomination. Neither shalt thou lie with any beast to defile thyself therewith: neither shall any woman stand before a beast to lie down thereto: it is confusion."

Mark 10:6-8, "But from the beginning of the creation God made them male and female. For this cause shall a man leave his father and mother and cleave to his wife; And they twain shall be one flesh: so, then they are no more twain, but one flesh."

Romans 1:27, "And likewise also the men, leaving the natural use of the woman, burned in their lust one toward another; men with men working that which is unseemly, and receiving in themselves that recompence of their error which was meet."

Genesis chapter 19, God destroyed Sodom and Gomorrah because of the abomination lifestyle of homosexuality and lesbianism.

WAKE UP!!!!!

JESUS CHRIST over everything!!!!!

Homosexuality/Lesbianism Is a Sin

Did you know that lesbianism and homosexuality is a sin??? These are demonic spirits that deceive and manipulate people into feeling/thinking that this is a way of life and that this is acceptable with God. Be not deceived. This way of living is an abomination unto God. LEVITICUS 18: 22-23, (King James Bible) "Thou shalt not lie with mankind, as with womankind; it is abomination. Neither shalt thou lie with any beast to defile thyself therewith: neither shall any woman stand before a beast to lie down thereto: it is confusion."

LEVITICUS 20:13, "If a man also lies with mankind, as he lieth with a woman, both of them have committed an abomination: they shall surely be put to death: their blood shall be upon them." God made female for the male and male for the female.

Genesis 2:21-24, "And the Lord God caused a deep sleep to fall upon Adam, and he slept: and he took one of his ribs and closed up the flesh instead thereof; And the rib, which the Lord God had taken from man, made he a woman, and brought her unto the man. And Adam said, this is now bone of my bones, and flesh of my flesh: she shall be called Woman, because she was taken out of Man. Therefore, shall a man leave his father and his mother, and shall cleave unto his wife; and they shall be one flesh."

Ref: ST. Mark 10:6 & 9, "But from the beginning of the creation God made them male and female. What therefore God hath joined together, let not man put asunder."

Be not deceived.... It is God's will that a husband and wife consist of a man and a woman, NOT male and male or female and female. Even in dating and relationships, this is also for male and female, NOT male & male, or female & female. Spread the truth, please do not die (either SPIRITUALY, because when you are in sin, you are absent from God...or PHYSICALLY, because the wages of sin are death) in your sins. There is a way to save yourself and to change your life around.

ACTS 2: 38-39, "Then Peter said unto them, Repent, and be baptized every one of you in the name of Jesus Christ for the remission of sins, and ye shall receive the gift of the Holy Ghost. For the promise is unto you, and to your children, and to all that are afar off, even as many as the Lord our God shall call".

Yes, REPENT from your sins...... Ask God's forgiveness and turn from your sins, but truly mean this in your hearts. You don't have to die in your sins. God will give you strength to overcome that form of lifestyle, thoughts and urges.

JAMES 4:7, "Submit yourselves therefore to God. Resist the devil, and he will flee from you." 2 CORINTHIANS 12:9, "And he said unto me, my grace is sufficient for thee: for my strength is made perfect in weakness. Most gladly therefore will I rather glory in my infirmities, that the power of Christ may rest upon me." God cannot lie, and his word will never fail....

ISAIAH 55:11, "So shall my word be that goeth forth out of my mouth: it shall not return unto me void, but it shall accomplish that which I please, and it shall prosper in the thing whereto I sent it."

Be not deceived, this lifestyle is not of God at all......... JESUS IS LORD................. Jesus loves you more than you know... JESUS the Living Word!!

What Is Faith

FAITH……….. What is it? How do you possess it?

HEBREWS 11:1, "Now faith is the substance of things hoped for, the evidence of things not seen." Faith is loyalty, belief, or reliance.

Faith is a practical expression of your confidence in God and his word (which is God, ST. JOHN 1:1-2, "In the beginning was the Word, and the Word was with God, and the Word was God. The same was in the beginning with God.") The law of the Kingdom of God is Faith.

The Word of God is the constitution of the Kingdom.

(KING JAMES BIBLE) ST. MATTHEW 6:33-34, "But seek ye first the kingdom of God, and his righteousness; and all these things shall be added unto you. Take therefore no thought for the morrow: for the things of itself. Sufficient unto the day is the evil thereof."

ROMANS 1:17, "For therein is the righteousness of God revealed from faith to faith: as it is written, "The just shall live by faith."

Faith is a prescription for living.

No Word, no Faith

Little Word, little Faith

Much Word, much Faith

If you are going to participate in the Kingdom, you need to get equipped. Let Faith equal the Word of God. So, if you don't know the Word of God, you don't know faith, and you don't know how to live.

What you are more developed in is what is going to be manifested. So, if you have more fear, then that is what's going to show up. If you have confidence, that is what's going to be manifested. Even though your circumstances change, don't you change your confidence in God, no matter what!!!!

When you have confidence in God, you are saying that you completely lean on or rely on God.

You are demonstrating trust which is an expression of your commitment to God.

HEBREWS 10:35, "Cast not away therefore your confidence, which hath great recompence of reward."

1 JOHN 5:14-15, "And this is the confidence that we have in him, that, if we ask any thing according to his will, he heareth us: And if we know that he hears us, whatsoever we ask, we know that we have the petitions that we desired of him." ST. MARK 11:24, "Therefore I say unto you, what things soever ye desire, when ye pray, believe that ye receive them, and ye shall have them."

EPHESIANS 6:16, "Above all, taking the shield of faith, wherewith ye shall be able to quench all the fiery darts of the wicked."

ROMANS 8:28, "And we know that all things work together for good to them that love God, to them who are the called according to his purpose."

ROMANS 10:17, "So then faith cometh by hearing, and hearing by the word of God."

The devil tries to deceive people with moorages, he wants people to be discouraged, depressed, stressed, pressured, and in oppression by what they are going through, but do not take your eyes off God, things are not what they look like. Remember God is able to do just what he said he will do.

2 CORINTHIANS 5:7, "For we walk by faith, not by sight:"

Ref: ROMANS 8:24, "For we are saved by hope: but hope that is seen is not hope: for what a man seeth, why doth he yet hope for?"

HEBREWS 11:6, "But without faith it is impossible to please him: for he that cometh to God must believe that he is, and that he is a rewarder of them that diligently seek him." We must first believe that God is able to do whatever we need him to do. Otherwise, why do you call on him if you do even believe he is able to do what you ask? You know, you do not have to have a whole lot of faith, but just a little. ST. MARK 11:22-24, "And Jesus answering saith unto them, Have faith in God. For verily I say unto you, that whosoever shall say unto this mountain, be thou removed, and be thou cast into the sea; and shall not doubt in his heart but shall believe that those things which he saith shall come to pass; he shall have whatsoever he saith. Therefore, I say unto you, what things soever ye desire, when ye pray, believe that ye receive them, and ye shall have them."

PSALMS 118:8, "It is better to trust in the Lord than to put confidence in man."

ISAIAH 55:11, "So shall my word be that goeth forth out of my mouth: it shall not return unto me void, but it shall accomplish that which I please, and it shall prosper in the thing whereto I sent it."

Trust in God, he is his Word, and he cannot fail. God is not a man that he shall lie, he is a spirit, and they that worship him, worship him in spirit and in truth. Jesus loves you more than you know............ JESUS the Living Word!!!!!!!!!!!!!!!

What Is Fear

What is FEAR?? It is terror, a feeling of agitation, anxiety caused by present or imminent danger, or to be afraid (filled with fear; frighten). It is an unpleasant (which means it is not joyous—there is no joy in it) strong emotion caused by expectation (something that you are expecting to happen that has not happened yet) or awareness (just being aware of danger or crime that's going on around perhaps in neighborhoods) of danger or anxious (worried, eagerly wishing) concern.

DO NOT LET FEAR BE MOTIVATION FOR DOING WHAT YOU DO!!!!! KNOW WHAT

FEAR BRINGS WITH IT…. (torment)

Fear is based on the past, FAITH is now.

Fear is the root of the matter; however, fear can show up in your life in many different forms. Forms of fear:

An Inferior attitude- Having an attitude where you think you are of lesser quality (nature or degree of excellence), of little importance, value, or merit.

Panic – Groundless fear (meaning having no foundation, groundless, baseless, invalid), anxiety, fright.

Nervous – Despite what people have been taught in school, on their jobs, or just by the world period, nervousness is a form of fear which is not of God. It means to be jumpy, spooky, troubled, concerned, worried, bothered.

Anxiety - Painful uneasiness of mind (this is a troubled mind that is accompanied by actual pain), nervousness, worry, stress, strain (excessive tension), apprehensive (viewing the future with anxiety).

Anger (what are you afraid of?), Insecurity (what are you insecure about, what are you fearing?), Worry (what are you troubled by that's got you bound by fear?), Competitive, and Jealous are all forms of fear.

Now the world would have you to believe that all these things are ok but the truth of the matter is that they are all forms of fear.

Fear is of the devil.

Fear is not of God, because God's word (which cannot lie) tells us this (when people take the time to read it--King James Version Bible)

2TIMOTHY 1:7 "For God hath not given us the spirit of fear; but of power, and of love and a sound mind."

Fear is not of God. Fear hath torment, and torment is not of God.

ST. JOHN 10:28 "And fear not them which kill the body but are not able to kill the soul: but rather fear him which is able to destroy both soul and body in hell."

We are not to fear man (flesh). A lot of times we walk around fearing others and for what????? We sometimes allow ourselves to be intimidated or feel threaten by what others say, how they act, or even what they do. God made man, so why would you fear the creation and not the Creator????

1 JOHN 4:4 "Ye are of God, little children, and have overcome them: because greater is he that is in you, than he that is in the world."

Ref: 1 john 5:4 "For whatsoever is born of God overcometh the world: and this is the victory that overcometh the world, even our faith."

When you are walking by faith, you have no fear. Now why is this, because.

ROMANS 1:17 talks about the just shall live by faith. We know that in HEBREWS 11:6 talks about, without faith it is impossible to please him, for he that cometh to God must believe that he is, and he is a rewarder of them that diligently seek him. When you walk in fear you are crippling yourself.

You remain in bondage because you limit yourself.... your life.... your success. Yes, fear is a spirit, but this fear spirit (because fear hath torment) begins to attack your mind...your way of thinking, and if you are not transformed by the renewing of your mind, from being in the word of God (ROMANS 12:1-3), you will crumble. In order to overcome fear, you first got to renew your mind in the word of God. Once you have this word in you, believing his word, begin to speak God's word into your life, upon your situations, and watch what happens. I do not care what you may be going through or what it looks like; continue believing and speaking God's word. You will notice that as you believe and speak God's word; notice how you will begin to stand on God's word. Things will begin to change and /or come to pass in your life. So, when fear comes upon you, give it the word of God and watch the salvation of the Lord step in. Remember God's word is sharper than any two-edge sword, so use it!!!!!!!!!!!!!!!! Watch the word of God change, fix, heal, separate, move, intervene, and set free whatever you are going through....... So, reflecting on 2 TIMOTHY 1:7....... (God hath not given us the Spirit of fear...... but of Power......)

A child of God ((born again believer, saved individual that has repented (to have a change of thought, turn from) of their sins and accepted Jesus Christ as their Lord and Savior)) that has the greater one dwelling within him/her, must realize just what they have......

Spirit: We were made in the image of God (Genesis 1:26-27). God is spirit (ST John 4:24), so we were made spirit after God. Now in II Timothy 1:7, God is speaking on his spirit, which is the Holy Ghost. Look at this closely, God did not give us (his saints) a spirit that is fearful, frighten, nervous, or of panic, inferior, or anxious, but God gave us (his saints) a spirit of power, love, and a sound mind. Spirit of Power: What do God mean when he says, he has given us (his saints) a spirit of Power? The Holy Ghost (which is God's spirit that we were given freely by God when we were born again and filled with his precious Holy Ghost), is a spirit of power.

-Ref: ST John 15:26 (King James Version Bible)

This talks about the Holy Ghost being a Comforter, the Spirit of Truth, and Shall testify of Jesus. Comfort – Means the act or an instance of consoling, freedom from pain, trouble, or anxiety, or encouragement.

Ref: ST John 16:7-15

This scripture talks about the Holy Ghost 1st Reproving the world of sin, and of righteousness, and of judgment (convicting the world where sin is concerned, convicting their hearts of sin, convicting the saints of God in regard to righteousness, in other words-when a saint ((someone that is born again or repented (turned from their sins or changed their way of thinking) and accepted Christ as their Savior and were baptized in Jesus name)) of God sin the Holy Ghost convicts our hearts in righteousness showing us that we are the righteousness of God and we are not supposed to behave that way, and of judgment because remember satan has already been judged and punished to the pits of hell, satan has no power (ST Juke 10:19-20) and cannot destroy you, that is why he can only attack in your life by interfering in your mind-set. Remember satan suggested a thought to Eve in the garden (Genesis 3:1-5) however, it was Eve who transgressed against her husband and Adam (her husband) who sinned against God (because God gave the commandment to the head of the house which was Adam and Adam made sure his house knew of the commandment and Eve displayed this when she said what she said to satan in Genesis 3:1-24), 2nd Guide you into all truth, 3rd Speak whatever he hears (so whatever the Holy Ghost hears from God is what he speaks to you (saints)), and 4th Show you things to come. So, we do not have to be afraid when we hear of what is happening or going to happen in the world, because the Holy Ghost will show us things to come.

Spirit of Love: The Holy Ghost is God's spirit,

(I John 4:8) this scripture is talking about God is love. So, God which is spirit, made us in his image, when we got born again, our spirit became one with God (1 Corinthians 6:17), Jesus sent us the Holy Ghost (ST John 15:26). Since God is love, his spirit is love then. God = his spirit, which = love.

Ref: (1 John 4:7-21)

1 John 4:18) this talks about there is no fear in Love. Perfect (flawless) love casteth out fear. There is no fear in Love and since God is love, there is no fear (concerning fear stated at the beginning of this flyer and the different forms of fear) in God. God, which is love, is perfect love.

If you say you got God, then you have Love and God which is Perfect Love, will cast out fear. Spirit of Sound Mind: Did you know that sound mind means self-discipline, or peace of mind or a mind free from fear or a mind-set that lines up with the word of God.

Jesus is Peace. We have peace in Jesus. ST John 14:27 and ST John 16:33

When we have a mind-set that lines up with the Word of God, then we have Peace, but when you have a mind-set that lines up with the world's way of thinking or a carnal mind-set, then you have tribulation = trouble=fear.

This is the spirit of power that God gave you, because your body is the temple of the Holy Ghost (ROMANS 6:19, "What? Know ye not that your body is the temple of the Holy Ghost, which is in you, which ye have of God, and ye are not your own.") Which is God's spirit dwelling in you? If you have God's spirit dwelling on the inside, you have power, by his spirit. (ST. LUKE 10:19, "Behold, I give unto you power to tread on serpents and scorpions, and over all the power of the enemy: and nothing shall by any means hurt you.") Through God's spirit you have power over all the power over the devil (ST Luke 10:19). Greater is the spirit of God that dwells on the inside of you, than the devil going to and fro in the world seeking whom he may devour. WOW…. look at JESUS…...

Again, we are talking about the spirit of God. So, through God's spirit, not only do you have power over all the power of the enemy, but you have a spirit of love. 1 JOHN 4:8, "He that loveth not knoweth not God; for God is love." God is love that is why you are able to love your neighbor as yourself. Through God you can forgive (truly forgive) and love your enemies, love those who talk about you, lie on you, mistreat you, hurt you, abuse you, and use you. God said in ROMANS 12:19 that vengeance is his. We are to pray for one another and provoke one another to love.

ROMANS 12:1-3 talks about being transformed by the renewing of your mind. In order for you to do this, you first got to get into God's word and learn of him. Read and see what his will is and what his will is for your life. ST. JOHN 16:33, "These things I have spoken unto you, that in me ye might have peace. In the world ye shall have tribulation: but he of good cheer; I have overcome the world." So, in Jesus you have peace, which brings us back to fear (which hath torment) is not of God. God tells you in his word what he gave you a spirit of. (2 CORITHIANS 3:17, "Now the Lord is that Spirit; and where the Spirit of the Lord is, there is liberty." Because you are in Christ, you are free from fear. Keep in mind, to be present with the Lord (being a hearer and doer of his word or being in his presence) and absent from sin (living a life that consist of anything outside the word of God)

HOW TO RECOGNIZE FEAR:
Understand where it comes from.
Realize it is an emotional attack.

You cannot do anything in the kingdom of darkness, which comes by fear and that works by selfishness.

HOW TO GET OUT OF FEAR:
Get in Love which =God I John 4:18

Understand that most fear comes from not knowing what's going to happen (It is essential or very very important that you(saints) trust the Holy Ghost to reveal to you what's to come)

Fear comes from feeling powerless over the future (your future is in your seed (the Word of God). So, sow the Word of God in your life (Joshua 1:8) there is a solution to every problem that you saint or not will ever face in your life, and it is in the Word of God, but you have got to stop being lazy and READ READ READ READ. A lot of people do not ever see change in their lives because they won't pick up the Word of God and read, study it, let it marinate in them and then obey it!!!!!!!!

Live by FAITH. Hear God's Word and receive God's FAITH. It is the Word of God that sets you FREE……….. so get in it!!!!!!! THE TIME IS NOW, NOT TOMORROW, FOR TOMORROW IS NOT PROMISED (ST Matthew 6:21-34), SO THE TIME IS NOW, if you want change then to get in the Word of God and observe or see what he will have you to do and do it!!!!!!

JESUS IS LORD…

Jesus loves you more than you know………… JESUS the Living Word!!!!!

Encouragement

THIS IS FOR YOU!!!!!!!!! (2 CHRONICLES 20:17)
Whatever you have been dealing with, going through on your job, in your marriage, in your family, in your relationship, concerning your health, in your friendships, with your schooling, in your mind, in making a serious decision, in any area in your life......the battle is not yours; it is the Lord's!!! God is going to show up and show out in your life!!!! All you must do is show up for the battle and STAND still and SEE the salvation of the Lord Jesus Christ!!!! Open your mouth.

BOLDLY and speak God's Word in EVERY area in your life!

Here are some study scriptures: PSALM 23, ISAIAH 53:4- 5, 2 CORINTHIANS 1: 3-4, 2 CHRONICLES 20:17, 2 CORINTHIANS 12:9, MARK 11:22-26, ROMANS 8:24-25, ROMANS 8:28------

Walk by Faith and not by sight. Do Not, I repeat Do Not be moved by what you see with the natural eye but walk by faith knowing that God has already took care of that situation. Stop trying to do it on your own, just give it to JESUS, and remember, when Jesus says yes, no one can say no. When Jesus opens that door, no man and nothing can close it!!!!!

Be blessed in the Lord and Savior Jesus Christ!!!!!

Repentance......

What is it, what does it mean to repent????

Repent means to feel regret, to change one's mind about......

Did you know that sin (anything that goes against the Word of God) is the ruin (destruction, annihilation, or waste) of the soul (mind, will and emotions because man is a spirit that possesses a soul and lives in a physical body) because sin leads death (Romans 6:23 "For the wages of sin is death; but the gift of God is eternal life through Jesus Christ our Lord.") You must make changes in your lifestyle; it is necessary for salvation (deliverance).... Yes, we are living in the last days, and while you still have time because tomorrow is not promised, repent (turn from your wicked ways) and accept Jesus as your Lord and Savior!!!!!

Matthew 24: 4:8

"And Jesus answered and said unto them, take heed that no man deceives you.

For many shall come in my name, saying, I am Christ; and shall deceive many. And ye shall hear of wars and rumors of wars: see that ye be not troubled: for all these things must come to pass, but the end is not yet.

For nation shall rise against nation, and kingdom against kingdom: and there shall be famines, and pestilences, and earthquakes, in divers' places.

All these are the beginning of sorrows.)

(2 Timothy 3: 1-7 " This know also, that in the last days perilous times shall come. For men shall be lovers of their own selves, covetous, boasters, proud, blasphemers, disobedient to parents, unthankful, unholy,

Without natural affection, trucebreakers, false accusers, incontinent, fierce, despisers of those that are good,

Traitors, heady, high-minded, lovers of pleasures more than lovers of God; Having a form of godliness but denying the power thereof: from such turn away. For of this sort are they which creep into houses, and lead captive silly women laden with sins, led away with divers' lusts, ever learning, and never able to come to the knowledge of the truth.)

1 John 2:18-19 " Little children, it is the last time: and as ye have heard that antichrist shall come, even now are there many antichrists; whereby we know that it is the last time.

They went out from us, but they were not of us; for if they had been of us, they would no doubt have continued with us: but they went out, that they might be made manifest that they were not all of us.

1 John 2:22-23 "Who is a liar but he that denieth that Jesus is the Christ? He is antichrist, that denieth the Father and the Son. Whosoever denieth the Son, the same hath not the Father: (but) he that acknowledgeth the Son hath the Father also.") Repentance....

1 John 3: 6-9 "Whosoever abideth in him sinneth not: whosoever sinneth hath not seen him, neither known him. Little children let no man deceive you: he that doeth righteousness is righteous, even as he is righteous.

He that committeth sin is of the devil; for the devil sinneth from the beginning. For this purpose, the Son of God was manifested, that he might destroy the works of the devil. Whosoever is born of God doth not commit sin; for his seed remaineth in him: and he cannot sin, because he is born of God."

Mark 16:16 "He that believeth and is baptized shall be saved; but he that believeth not shall be damned."

Matthew 38: 19 "Go ye therefore, and teach all nations, baptizing them in the name of the Father, and of the Son, and of the Holy Ghost."

John 3: 3-6 "Jesus answered and said unto him, Verily, verily, I say unto thee, except a man be born again, he cannot see the kingdom of God.

Nicodemus saith unto him, how can a man be born when he is old? can he enter the second time into his mother's womb, and be born? Jesus answered, Verily, verily, I say unto thee, except a man be born of water and of the Spirit, he cannot enter into the kingdom of God. That which is born of the flesh is flesh; and that which is born of the Spirit is spirit."

Acts 2: 38-39 "Then Peter said unto them, Repent, and be baptized every one of you in the name of Jesus Christ for the remission of sins, and ye shall receive the gift of the Holy Ghost. For the promise is unto you, and to your children, and to all that are afar off, even as many as the Lord our God shall call."

2 Chronicles 7:14 " If my people, which are called by my name, shall humble themselves, and pray, and seek my face, and turn from their wicked ways; then will I hear from heaven, and will forgive their sin, and will heal their land

Repentance does not have to be hard. If you don't know where to start, repeat after me Lord Jesus I repent of my sins, forgive me Lord, I believe that Jesus died on the cross and rose again for me, I accept you as my Savior, come into my life Jesus and save me. I ask you Father in Jesus name to fill me with your Holy Spirit that I might speak with other tongues as you spirit gives me utterance.

It is just that easy!

When you repent you take responsibility and choose now to live according to the Word of God. Now it is time to develop a relationship with God. Start by studying his Word to learn of him and know how he would have you to live. God said if you draw close to him, he will draw close to you.

(James 4:8 "Draw nigh to God, and he will draw nigh to you. Cleanse your hands, ye sinners; and purify your hearts, ye double minded.")

Just think if you have been living that way for so long and getting those results why not try it Jesus's way and have better results 😊!!!!!!

There is a heaven and there is a hell......which will you choose to live eternally at????

Consequences

There are **consequences** for your actions……

You can ask someone to pray for you but if your ways and mindset has not changed, it can determine what consequences will follow.

(example): Numbers chapter 14 talks about how God was going to cause negative consequences to come upon Israel due to their disobedience and unbelief, but Moses intervened on behalf of this rebellious nation and as a result, God show mercy (he pardoned), but the consequences of them not changing their mindset and repenting and turning from sin, they would not get to see the promised land, their children (who were not at the age of accountability) would but the adults (who were at the age of accountability) would not. They died in the wilderness due to disobedience and unbelief.

So…….what am I saying, you are responsible for your actions, thoughts, and the words that come out of your mouth. There are consequences for every action be it good or bad.

Ref: Deuteronomy chapter 28.

Sin leads to death.

James 1:13-17, " Let no man say when he is tempted, I am tempted of God: for God cannot be tempted with evil, neither tempteth he any man: But every man is tempted, when he is drawn away of his own lust, and enticed. Then when lust hath conceived, it bringeth forth sin: and sin, when it is finished, bringeth forth death. Do not err, my beloved brethren. Every good gift and every perfect gift is from above, and cometh down from the Father of lights, with whom is no variableness, neither shadow of turning."

1 John 5:16-20, "If any man see his brother sin a sin which is not unto death, he shall ask, and he shall give him life for them that sin not unto death. There is a sin unto death: I do not say that he shall pray for it. All unrighteousness is sin: and there is a sin not unto death. We know that whosoever is born of God sinneth not; but he that is begotten of God keepeth himself, and that wicked one toucheth him not. And we know that we are of God, and the whole world lieth in wickedness. And we know that the Son of God is come, and hath given us an understanding, that we may know him that is true, and we are in him that is true, even in his Son Jesus Christ.

This is the true God, and eternal life."

Now is the opportunity to repent and turn from your evil ways and renew your mind in the Word of good (studying the word of God to see how God would have you to live, what he is saying, what ways and actions and words are acceptable of him and what he considers to be an abomination)

You may not have another chance!!!!!

Every man has a will. You can ask a Christian to pray for you but if you do not change your ways.... you will face the consequences.

Please hear this warning and stop living the way you have been. God is not pleased. We have to be mindful what we watch (allow our eyes to see), hear (allow our ears to hear), because all of that can have an effect on our mindset. Study the Word daily without ceasing and build yourself up. You will not be able to stand for what's to come without the Word of God. Eat healthy and meditate in his Word. 😊

You must take care of the temple of the Holy Ghost (this is your physical body). (1 Corinthians chapter 6), God's spirit dwells in your body (for Christians), build your immune system. Your health has to be important to you.

Divination/Witchcraft

Divination is the art or practice of using omens or magic, powers to foretell the future.

So yes everyone, physics is not of God, this is a form of witchcraft. Keep in mind, anything that does not line up with the Word of God, is not of God.

Have you heard or seen people use the month of someone's birthday and try to say that they must be of this sign or that, well, this too is a form of witchcraft. This is not of God. Saints listen up, your true identity is in the Word of God. If you ever wanted to know how your spirit looks, just meditate in the Word of God, because spiritual things go with spiritual things. For those that are not save, repent and be baptized in the name of Jesus, and ye shall receive the gift of the Holy Ghost (which is God's spirit)
Idolatry is the worship of a physical object as a false god. Now false gods can consist of anything. Whatever you give more of your time to, other than Jesus Christ, is a false god. It can be work, school, people, TV, music, whatever……anything or one that you give more of your time to than the time you spend with God is an idol. And yes, when people make, or have images of animals, people, objects, or whatever, and bow down before them, or worship them, these are false gods, and you are practicing in witchcraft.
1 SAMUEL 15:23, "For rebellion is as the sin of witchcraft, and stubbornness is as iniquity and idolatry. Because thou hast rejected the word of the Lord, he hath also rejected thee from being king."

Ref: DEUTERONOMY 18:10-13, "There shall not be found among you anyone that maketh his son or his daughter to pass through the fire, or that useth divination, or an observer of times, or an enchanter, or a witch, Or a charmer, or a consulter with familiar spirits, or a wizard, or a necromancer. For all of these things are an abomination unto the Lord: and because of these abominations the Lord thy God doth drive them out from before thee. Thou shalt be perfect with the Lord thy God."

GALATIANS 5:19-21, "Now the works of the flesh are manifest, which are these; Adultery, fornication, uncleanness, lasciviousness, Idolatry, witchcraft, hatred, variance, emulations, wrath, strife, seditions, heresies, envyings, murders, drunkenness, revellings, and such like: of the which I tell you before, as I have also told you in time past, that they which do such things shall not inherit the kingdom of God."

REVELATIONS 22:14-15, "Blessed are they that do his commandments, that they may have right to the tree of life and may enter in through the gates into the city. For without are dogs, and sorcerers, and whoremongers, and murderers, and idolaters, and whosoever loveth and maketh a lie."

Now we see hear that rebellion is like the sin of witchcraft, so when people rebel against God's word, they are doing witchcraft.

EXODUS 20:3-5, "Thou shalt have no other gods, before me. Thou shalt not make unto thee any graven image, or any likeness of anything that is in heaven above, or that is in the earth beneath, or that is in the water under the earth: Thou shalt not bow down thyself to them, nor serve them: for I the Lord thy God am a jealous God, visiting the iniquity of the fathers upon the children unto the third and forth generation of them that hate me; And shewing mercy unto thousands of them that love me, and keep my commandments."

Jesus loves you more than you know............ JESUS the Living Word!

Consulting God

Without **consulting God**, you will always make the wrong decision!!!!
II Chronicles chapter 20
V: 1- "It came to pass after this also, that the children of Moab, and the children of Ammon, and with them other beside the Ammonites, came against Jehoshaphat to battle."
We see moab (a nation of people), the children of ammon (another nation of people), and other coming against Jehoshaphat to battle. So not only does Jehoshaphat have two kinds of people coming against him but other (another kind of people) also.
V: 2- "Then there came some that told Jehoshaphat, saying, there cometh a great multitude against thee from beyond the sea on this side Syria; and behold, they be in Hazazontamar, which is Engedi." So, we see here that a warning of the war or storm or tribulation is being told to Jehoshaphat. Even the location of the great host (multitude).
We see that this was a great multitude coming against him. Now for these that came and warned him of this great multitude apparently, this great multitude had to out-number Jehoshaphat and his army.
V: 3- "And Jehoshaphat feared, and set himself to seek the Lord, and proclaimed a fast throughout all Judah."
Now check out what Jehoshaphat did immediately when he got word of this great multitude that was coming up against him. Jehoshaphat set himself to seek the Lord and proclaimed (declare) a fast throughout all Judah. Wow look at this, so Jehoshaphat consulted God first. When he got word of his approaching tribulation, he sought God first!!!! He did

not consult flesh (man), but instead he consulted the one who is able to change his situation. And not only that but he proclaimed a fast, not just for himself but with all of Judah. He didn't panic and have self-work (try to work it out through your own abilities), trying to figure out what to do or looking unto others. He instead put his TRUST and CONFIDENCE in the ALMIGHTY GOD. And everyone was on one accord.

Ref: (s)

Again, you see someone else in the mist of tribulation, consulting GOD first and proclaiming a fast.

Ezra 8:21,23, "Then I proclaimed a fast there, at the river of Ahava, that we might afflict ourselves before out God, to seek of him a right way for us, and for our little ones, and for all our substance. So, we fasted and besought our God for this: and he was intreated of us."

Joel 1:14, "Sanctify ye a fast, call a solemn assembly, gather the elders and all the inhabitants of the land into the house of the Lord your God, and cry unto the Lord,"

Jonah 3:1-10, "And the word of the Lord came unto Jonah the second time, saying, Arise, go unto Nineveh, that great city, and preach unto it the preaching that I bid thee. So, Jonah arose, and went unto Nineveh, according to the word of the Lord. Now Nineveh was an exceeding great city of three days' journey. And Jonah began to enter into the city a day's journey, and he cried, and said, yet forty days, and Nineveh shall be overthrown. So, the people of Nineveh believed God, and proclaimed a fast, and put on sackcloth, from the greatest of them even to the least of them. For word came unto the king of Nineveh, and he arose from his throne, and he laid his robe from him, and covered him with sackcloth, and sat in ashes. And he caused it to be proclaimed and published through Nineveh by the decree of the king and his nobles, saying, let neither man nor beast, herd nor flock, taste any thing: let them not feed, nor drink water: But let man and beast be covered with sackcloth, and cry mightily unto God: yea, let them turn everyone from his evil way, and from the violence that is in their hands. Who can tell if God will turn and repent, and turn away from his fierce anger, that we perish not? And God saw their works, that they turned from their evil way; and God repented of the evil, that he had said that he would do unto them; and he did it not."

V: - 6, "And said, O Lord God of our father, art not thou God in heaven? And rulest not thou over all the kingdoms of the heathen? And in thine hand is there not power and might, so that none is able to withstand thee?"

Ref: (s)

Joshua 2:9-11, "And she said unto the men, I know that the Lord hath given you the land, and that your terror is fallen upon us, and that all the inhabitants of the land faint because of you. For we have heard how the Lord dried up the water of the Red sea for you, when ye came out of Egypt; a what ye did unto the two kings of the Amorites, that were on the other side Jordan, Sihon and Og, whom ye utterly destroyed. And as soon as we had heard these things, our hearts did melt, neither did they remain any more courage in any man, because of you: for the Lord your God, he is God in heaven above, and in earth beneath. "

Now here, Jehoshaphat speaks to God and reminds God of his awesomeness, his power, and his might.

V:7-9, "Art not thou our God, who didst drive out the infabitants of this land before thy people Israel, and gavest it to the seed of Abraham thy friend forever? And they dwelt therein and have built thee a sanctuary therein for thy name, saying, If, when evil cometh upon us, as the sword, judgment, or pestilence, or famine, we stand before this house, and in thy presence, (for thy name is in this house,) and cry unto thee in our affliction, then thou wilt hear and help."

Again, he (Jehoshaphat) remembers what God has done before and how merciful and awesome God is. At the end of verse 9, Jehoshaphat says something that is so true, he says to God that when they cry unto God, he will hear and help.

V:10-12, "And now, behold, the children of Ammon and Moab and mount Seir, whom thou wouldest not let Israel invade, when they came out of the land of Egypt, but they turned from them, and destroyed them not; Behold, I say, how they reward us, to vome to cast us out of thy possession, which thou hast given us to inherit. O our God, wilt thou not judge them? For we have no might against this great company that cometh against us; neither know we what to do: but our eyes are upon thee."

Again, he carries on remembering what God did before. Then he talks about how this people have come up against them, and they did not know what to do, however, their eyes were on the Lord.

So, even when through the natural eye, could not see a way out, they instead put their eyes upon the Lord!!!

V:14, "Then upon Jahaziel the son of Zechariah, the son of Benaiah, the son of Jeiel, the sonof Mattaniah, a Levite of the sons of Asaph, came the spirit of the Lord in the midst of the congregation.

Now because all of Judah were on one accord, and remember, where two or three are gathered together on earth in his

name (Jesus), there he is in the mist of them. So as a result, the spirit of the Lord came in the mist of the congregation.
V:15, "An he said, Hearken ye, all Judah, and ye inhabitants of Jerusalem, and thou King Jehoshaphat, Thus saith the Lord unto you, Be not afraid nor dismayed by reason of this great multitude; for the battle is not yours, but God's."
God speaks and tells them not to be afraid or dismayed (discouraged), because of the multitude, because the battle is not theirs, but the Lord.

> Ref: Deuteronomy 1:29-30, "Then I said unto you, Dread not, neither be afraid of them. The Lord your God which goeth before you, he shall fight for you, according to all that he did for you in Egypt before your eyes;
> Exodus 14:13-14, "And Moses said unto the people, Fear ye not, stand still, and see the salvation of the Lord, which he will shew to you to-day: for the Egyptians whom ye have seen to-day, ye shall see them again no more forever. The Lord shall fight for you, and ye shall hold your peace. "

V: 16-17, "Tomorrow go ye down against them: behold, they come up by the cliff of Ziz; and ye shall find them at the end of the brook, before the wilderness of Jeruel. Ye shall not need to fight in this battle: set yourselves, stand ye still, and see the salvation of the Lord with you, O Judah and Jerusalem: fear not, nor e dismayed; tomorrow go out against them: for the Lord will be with you."
God tell them where they shall find the great multitude that was coming up against them, God tells them to stand still and see the salvation of the Lord.

> Ref: Numbers 14:9, "Only rebel not ye against the Lord, neither fear ye the people of the land; for they are bread for us: their defence is departed from them, and the Lord is with us: fear them not."

Deuteronomy 20:3-4, "And shall say unto them, Hear, O Israel, ye approach this day unto battle against your enemies: let not your hearts faint, fear not, and do not tremble, either be ye terrified because of them; For the Lord your God is he that goeth with you, to fight for you against your enemies, to save you."

V: 18, "And Jehoshaphat bowed his head with his face to the ground: and all Judah and the inhabitants of Jerusalem fell before the Lord, worshipping the Lord."

They then worshipped God.

V:19, "And the Levites, of the children of the Kohathires, and of the children of the Korhites, stood up to praise the Lord God of Israel with a loud voice on high."

They praised God.

V:20, "And they rose early in the morning, and went forth into the wilderness of Tekoa: and as they went forth, Jehoshaphat stood and said, hear me, O Judah, and ye inhabitants of Jerusalem; Believe in the Lord your God, so shall ye be established; believe his prophets, so shall ye prosper."

As they go early in the morning where God told them to find them, Jehoshaphat tells the people to believe in the Lord, and they shall be established (upheld), also to believe God's prophets, and they shall prosper (have success).

V:21, "And when he had consulted with the people, he appointed singers unto the Lord, and that should praise the beauty of holiness, as they went out before the army, and to say, Praise the Lord; for his mercy endureth forever."

They praise God for already solving the matter before it was done in the natural realm. Jehoshaphat appoints singers to give praise to God.

> Ref: I Chronicles 16:34, "O give thanks unto the Lord; for he is good; for his mercy endureth forever."

Psalms 136:1, "O Give thanks unto the Lord; for he is good: for his mercy endureth forever."
V:22-23, "And when they began to sing and to praise, the Lord set ambushements against the children of Ammon, Moab, and mount Seir, which were come against Judah; and they were smitten. For the children of Ammon and Moab stood up against the inhabitants of mount Seir, utterly to slay and destroy them: and when they had made an end of the inhabitants of Seir, everyone helped to destroy another."
And because they trusted in God, because the praised God, he took care of their enemies. The enemies killed off one another.
V: 24, "And when Judah came toward the watch tower in the wilderness, they looked unto the multitude, and behold, they were dead bodies fallen to the earth, and none escaped."
Judah beholds the dead bodies of all their enemies.
V:25, "And when Jehoshaphat and his people came to take away the spoil of them, they found among them in abundance both riches with the dead bodies, and precious jewels, which they stripped off for themselves, more than they could carry away: and they were three days in gathering of the spoil, it was so much."
God blessing exceedingly, abundantly above all they could ask or think three days it took them to gather what God had abundantly supplied.
So, everyone, we see II CHRONICLES chapter 20:6 talks about how Jehoshaphat begin with adoration (worship) toward God.
He reminded God of his promises,
Brought forth his problem to God.
And asked for help.
Then thanked God for the answer even before it came

Lack of Knowledge

HOSEA 4:6, "My people are destroyed for **lack of knowledge**: because thou hast rejected knowledge, I will also reject thee, that thou shalt be no priest to me: seeing thou hast forgotten the law of the God, I will also forget thy children.

Ref: ISAIAH 5:13, "Therefore my people are gone into captivity, because they have no knowledge: and their honourable men are famished, and their multitude dried up with thirst." Hello everyone, I want to touch on some things today that perhaps you either did not know, or knew little of......

II PETER 3:9, "The Lord is not slack concerning his promise, as some men count slackness; but is longsuffering to us-ward, not willing that any should perish, but that all should come to repentance."

God does not want anyone to have to go to hell and live-in torment for eternity. God wants everyone to come to the knowledge of truth.

ROMANS 6:23, "For the wages of sin is death; but the gift of God is eternal life through Jesus Christ our Lord"

Everyone must know that the payment that you receive for living in sin is

death. Now either that is death spiritually ((meaning to be spiritually cut off from God and his provisions (providing)) or physically ((meaning to die off of this earth in your sins having not repented of them----destination hell))

ACTS chapter 2 verses 38-39, "Then Peter said unto them, Repent, and be baptized every one of you in the name of Jesus Christ for the remission of sins, and ye shall receive the gift of the Holy Ghost. For the promise is unto you, and to your children, and to all that are afar off, even as many as the Lord our God shall call."

ST. JOHN chapter 3 verses 1-5, "There was a man of the Pharisees, named Nicodemus, a ruler of the Jews: The same came to Jesus by night, and said unto him, Rabbi, we know that thou art a teacher come from God: for no man can do these miracles that thou doest, except God be with him. Jesus answered and said unto him, Verily, verily, I say unto thee, except a man be born again, he cannot see the kingdom of God. Nicodemus saith unto him, how can a man be born when he is old? Can he enter the second time into his mother's womb, and be born? Jesus answered, Verily, verily, I say unto thee, except a man be born of water and of the Spirit, he cannot enter into the kingdom of God."

What it means to be saved/born again, is

> 1st accepting the Lord Jesus as your Lord and Savior (believing in your heart that Jesus is the son of God and they are one. Yes JESUS IS GOD.- 1John 5:7, "For there are three that bear record in heaven, the Father, the Word, and the Holy Ghost: and these three are one" –also PHILIPPIANS 2:9-11, "Wherefore God also hath highly exalted him, and given him a name which is above every name: That at the name of Jesus every knee should bow, of things in heaven, and things in earth, and things under the earth; And that every tongue should confess that Jesus Christ is Lord, to the glory of God the Father.")
>
> 2nd repenting for your sins (which means asking for forgiveness of all your sins from God and stopping and turning from them.)
>
> 3rd being baptized in the Name of Jesus,
>
> 4th then tarrying for the Holy Ghost (which means receiving God's spirit in you and speaking in other tongues as the Spirit of God gives you utterance)

Next, I would like to talk about, what an acquaintance of mine spoke about yesterday, <u>TATTOOS</u>.......
LEVITICUS 19:28, "Ye shall not make any cuttings in your flesh for the dead or print any marks upon you: I am the Lord.
> Ref: DEUTERONOMY 14:1, "Ye are the children of the Lord your God: ye shall not cut yourselves, nor make any baldness between your eyes for the dead,"

LEVITICUS 21:5, "They shall not make baldness upon their head, neither shall they shave off the corner of their beard, nor make any cuttings in their flesh."
What these scriptures are saying is do not cut your bodies for the dead or put tattoo marks on yourselves. Do not cut yourselves or shave the front of your heads for the dead. Continue.........
This, however, is also referring to priest, that they must not shave their heads or shave off the edges of their beards or cut their bodies. They must be holy to their God and must not profane the name of their God.
 Now, if you already have tattoos and voluntarily will not or at the moment cannot afford to remove them, as long as you repent, God will not hold that against you. God Judges the heart of man (which is his spirit, the intentions of the heart). 1 Thessalonians 5:23, "And the very God of peace sanctify you wholly; and I pray God your whole spirit and soul and body be preserved blameless unto the coming of our Lord Jesus Christ."
Man is a Spirit, who possesses a Soul (mind, will, emotions, personality, and countenance) and lives in a physical Body.
You do not have a spirit; you are a spirit. Your body does not possess a soul; your body has a brain.
Genesis 1:26-27, "And God said, let us make man in our image after our likeness: and let them have dominion over the fish of the sea, and over the fowl of the air, and over the

cattle, and over all the earth, and over every creeping thing that creepeth upon the earth. So, God created man in his own image, in the image of God created he him; male and female created he them." Genesis 2:7, "And the Lord God formed man of the dust of the ground and breathed into his nostrils the breath of life; and man became a living soul."
ST. John 4:24, "God is a Spirit: and they that worship him must worship him in spirit and in truth."

When Trouble Comes

When Trouble Comes, What Do You Do First???
The Answer: Seek God First!!!!!!!!
No matter what bad news you may receive, or what negative situation may occur in your life, let your first reaction be to set your face to the Lord first!!!!
DO NOT I repeat DO NOT react out of fear....
Do not try to handle the situation out of your own abilities (which by the way are limited, because YOU
　((spirit-being dwelling in flesh (King James Bible) 1 Thessalonians 5:23, "And the very God of peace sanctify you wholly; and I pray God your whole spirit and soul and body be preserved blameless unto the coming of our Lord Jesus Christ."
Man is a Spirit, who possesses a Soul (mind, will, emotions, personality, and countenance) and lives in a physical Body.
You do not have a spirit; you are a spirit. Your body does not possess a soul; your body has a brain.))
can only do so much, but with God nothing is impossible!!!
Matthew 19:26, 'But Jesus beheld them, and said unto them, with men this is impossible; but with God all things are possible.'
Luke 1:37, 'For with God nothing shall be impossible.'
Steps in how to set your face to God....
Come to God which is Jesus Christ ((
I JOHN 5:7, "For there are three that bear record in heaven, the Father, the Word, and the Holy Ghost: and these three are one" ...
JOHN 1:1-5, "In the beginning was the Word, and the Word was with God, and the Word was God. The same was in the

beginning with God. All things were made by him; and without him was not anything made that was made. In him was life; and the life was the light of men. And the light shineth in darkness; and the darkness comprehended it not."

DEUTERONOMY 4:39 "Know therefore this day, and consider it in thine heart, that the Lord he is God in heaven above and upon the earth beneath: there is none else."

PHILIPPIANS 2:10-11, "That at the name of Jesus every knee should bow, of things in heaven, and things in the earth, and things under the earth; and that every tongue should confess that Jesus Christ is Lord, to the glory of God the Father."

Yes, God is the Father, and Jesus is the only begotten son of God, they are one, because God is in Jesus and Jesus is in God. The Word (which is Jesus) came down in the form of flesh and dwelt among us.))

With praise.

Come before God with praise!!!

So, before you start to react to the bad news or negative situations, just start to praise God for who he is…

Psalm 100:2&4, 'Serve the Lord with gladness: come before his presence with singing. Enter into his gates with thanksgiving, and into his courts with praise be thankful unto him and bless his name.'

Start to remind God of who he is (now keep in mind that we are talking about God here and him being God does not need to be reminded of who he is because he already knows). However, when we come before God and begin to remind him of who he is and what he has done, is doing, and going to do. What we are doing is acknowledging and recognizing that he is God alone, there is none else, and we have accepted him as our Lord and Savior, and we are reverencing (honoring and respecting) God.

Genesis 17:1-2, 'And when A-bram was ninety years old and nine, the Lord appeared to A-bram, and said unto him, I am the Almighty God; walk before me, and be thou perfect. And I will make my covenant between me and thee, and will multiply thee exceedingly.'
Psalm 23:1, 'The Lord is my shepherd; I shall not want.
Psalm 27:1, 'The Lord is my light and my salvation; whom shall I fear? the Lord is the strength of my life; of whom shall I be afraid?'
Now here in this verse, light = sight (this is how your able to see beyond seeing) or guide, and salvation = deliverance
2 Corinthians 1:3-4, 'Blessed be God, even the Father of our Lord Jesus Christ, the Father of mercies, and the God of all comfort, Who comforteth us in all our tribulation, that we may be able to comfort them which are in any trouble, by the comfort wherewith we ourselves are comforted of God.'
Exodus 14:18-30, 'And the Egyptians shall know that I am the Lord, when I have gotten me honour upon Pharaoh, upon his chariots, and upon his horsemen. And the angel of God, which went before the camp of Israel, removed and went behind them; and the pillar of the cloud went from before their face, and stood behind them: And it came between the camp of the Egyptians and the camp of Israel; and it was a cloud and darkness to them, but it gave light by night to these: so that the one came not near the other all the night. And Moses stretched out his hand over the sea; and the Lord caused the sea to go back by a strong east wind all the night, and made the sea dry land, and the waters were divided. And the children of Israel went into the midst of the sea upon the dry ground: and the waters were a wall unto them on their right hand, and on their left. And the Egyptians pursued, and went in after them to the midst of the sea, even all Pharaoh's horses, his chariots, and his horsemen. And it came to pass, that in the morning watch the Lord looked unto the host of

the Egyptians through the pillar of fire and of the cloud, and troubled the host of the Egyptians, and took off their chariot wheels, that they drave them heavily: so that the Egyptians said, let us flee from the face of Israel; for the Lord fighteth for them against the Egyptians. And the Lord said unto Moses, Stretch out thine hand over the sea, that the waters may come again upon the Egyptians, upon their chariots, and upon their horsemen. And Moses stretched forth his hand over the sea, and the sea returned to his strength when the morning appeared; and the Egyptians fled against it; and the Lord overthrew the Egyptians in the midst of the sea. And the waters returned, and covered the chariots, and the horsemen, and all the host of Pharaoh that came into the sea after them; there remained not so much as one of them. But the children of Israel walked upon dry land in the midst of the sea; and the waters were a wall unto them on their right hand, and on their left. Thus, the Lord saved Israel that day out of the hand of the Egyptians; and Israel saw the Egyptians dead upon the seashore.'

Luke 8:43-48, 'And a woman having an issue of blood twelve years, which had spent all her living upon physicians, neither could be healed of any. Came behind him and touched the border of his garment: and immediately her issue of blood stanched. And Jesus said, who touched me? When all denied, Peter and they that were with him said, Master, the multitude throng thee and press thee, and sayest thou, who touched me? And Jesus said, somebody hath touched me: for I perceive that virtue is gone out of me. And when the woman saw that she was not hid, she came trembling, and falling down before him, she declared unto him before all the people for what because she had touched him, and how she was healed immediately. And he said unto her, Daughter, be of good comfort: thy faith hath made thee whole; go in peace.'

Now there are countless examples in the bible where God has provided, healed, set free, delivered, comforted, saved, given wisdom to, etc..
The next step in seeking God's face is <u>FASTING!!!!</u>
2 Chronicles 20:1-30,
'It came to pass after this also, that the children of Moeb, and the children of Ammon, and with them other beside the Ammonites, came against Jehoshaphat to battle. Then there came some that told Jehoshaphat, saying, there cometh a great multitude against thee from beyond the sea on this side Syria; and behold, they be in Hazazontamar, which is Engedi. And Jehoshaphat feared, and set himself to seek the Lord, and proclaimed a fast throughout all Judah. And Judah gathered themselves together, to ask help of the Lord: even out of all the cities of Judah they came to seek the Lord. And Jehoshaphat stood in the congregation of Judah and Jerusalem, in the huse of the Lord, before the new court, and said, O Lord God of our fathers, art not thou God in heaven? And rulest not thou over all the kingdoms of the heathen? And in thine hand is there not power and might, so that none is able to withstand thee? Art not thou our God, who didst drive out the inhabitants of this land before thy people Israel, and gavest it to the seed of Abraham thy friend forever? And they dwelt therein and have built thee a sanctuary therein for thy name, saying, If, when evil cometh upon us, as the sword, judgment, or pestilence, or famine, we stand before this house, and in thy presence, (for thy name is in this house,) and cry unto thee in our affliction, then thou wilt hear and help. And now, behold, the children of Ammon and Moab and mount Seir, whom thou wouldest not let Israel invade, when they came out of the land of Egypt, but they turned from them, and destroyed them not; Behold, I say, how they reward us, to come to cast us out of thy possession, which thou hast given us to inherit. O our God, wilt thou not judge

them? For we have no might against this great company that cometh against us; neither know we what to do: but our eyes are upon thee. And all Judah stood before the Lord, with their little ones, their wives, and their children. Then upon Jahaziel the son os Zechariah, the son of Benaiah, the son of Jeiel, the son of Mattaniah, a Levite of the sons of Asaph, came the Spirit of the Lord in the midst of the congregation; And he said, Hearken ye, all Judah, and ye inhabitants of Jerusalem and thou king Jehoshaphat, Thus saith the Lord unto you, Be not afraid nor dismayed by reason of this great multitude; for the battle is not yours but God's. Tomorrow go ye down against them: behold they come up by the cliff of Ziz; and ye shall find them at the end of the brook, before the wilderness of Jeruel. Ye shall not need to fight in this battle: set yourselves, stand ye still, and see the salvation of the Lord with you. O Judah and Jerusalem: fear not, nor be dismayed; tomorrow go out against them: for the Lord will be with you. And Jehoshaphat bowed his head with his face to the ground: and all Judah and the inhabitants of Jerusalem fell before the Lord, worshipping the Lord. And the Levites, of the children of Kohathites, and of the children of the Korhites, stood up to praise the Lord God of Israel with a loud voice on high. And they rose early in the morning, and went forth into the wilderness, of Tekoa: and as they went forth, Jehoshaphat stood and said, Hear me, O Jerusalem; Believe in the Lord your God, so shall ye be established; believe his prophets, so shall ye prosper. And when he had consulted with the people, he appointed singers unto the Lord, and that should praise the beauty of holiness, as they went out before the army, and to say, Praise the Lord; for his mercy endureth forever. And when they began to sing and to praise, the Lord set ambushments against the children of Ammon, Moab, and mount Seir, which were come against Judah; and they were smitten. For the children of Ammon and Moab stood up against the inhabitants of mount Seir, utterly to slay and destroy them: and when they had made an end of the inhabitants of Seir, everyone helped to destroy another, And when Judah came toward the watch tower in the wilderness, they looked unto the multitude, and, behold, they were dead bodies fallen to the earth, and none escaped. And when Jehoshaphat and his people came to take away the spoil of them, they found among them in abundance both riches with the dead bodies, and precious jewels, which they stripped off for themselves, more than they could carry away: and they were three days in gathering of the spoil, it was so much. And on the fourth day they assembled themselves in the valley of Berachah; for there they blessed the Lord: therefore, the name of the same place was called, The valley of Berachah, unto this day. Then they returned, every man of Judah and Jerusalem, and Jehoshaphat in the forefront of them, to go again to Jerusalem with joy; for the Lord had made them to rejoice over their enemies. And they came to Jerusalem with psalteries and harps and trumpets unto the house of the Lord. And the fear of God was on all the kingdoms of those countries, when they had heard that the Lord fought against the enemies of Israel.'

So, what happened here in the case of Jehoshaphat the king of Judah......the moment he received bad news that certain cities were gathering together to come up against him, what did he do????

The bible says he feared (for fear had come upon him in hearing the bad news), and set himself to seek the Lord, and proclaimed a **FAST**!!!!

So, he did not run and try to fix the problem himself,

He did not go find another human to fix the problem,

Instead, he sought the problem solver!!!!!

Let's look at another example of fasting in the bible.

Daniel 1:5, 8-16

And the king appointed them a daily provision of the king's meat, and of the wine which he drank: so nourishing them three years, that at the end thereof they might stand before the king. But Dainel purposed in his heart that he would not defile himself with the portion of the king's meat, nor with the wine which he drank: therefore, he requested of the prince of the eunuchs that he might not defile himself. Now God had brought Daniel into favour and tender love with the prince of the eunuchs. And the prince of the eunuchs said unto Daniel, I fear my lord the king, who hath appointed your meat and your drink: for why should he see your faces worse liking than the children which are of your sort? Then shall ye make me endanger my head to the king. Then said Daniel to Melzar, whom the prince of the eunuchs had set over Daniel, Hananiah, Mishael, and Azariah, Prove thy servants, I beseech thee, ten days; and let them give us pulse to eat, and water to drink. Then let our countenances be looked upon before thee, and the countenance of the children that eat of the portion of the king's meat: and as thou seest, deal with thy servants. So he consented to them in this matter, and proved them ten days. And at the end of then days their countenances appeared fairer and fatter in flesh than all the children which did eat the portion of the king's meat. Thus Melzar took away the portion of their meat, and the wine that they should drink; and gave them pulse.'
Esther ch: 3-5
Ch: 5 verses 7, 16
'And Mordecai told him of all that had happened unto him, and the sum of the money that Haman had promised to pay to the king's treasuries for the Jews, to destroy them. Go, gather together all the Jews that are present in Shushan, and fast ye for me, and neither eat nor drink three days, night or day: I also and my maidens will fast likewise; and so will I go

in unto the king, which is not according to the law: and if I perish, I perish.'

So again, we see here other examples of fasting for deliverance or an answer or wisdom.

The next thing you want to do is WORSHIP!!!

Even before you receive from God what you are seeking, worship him for already handling the matter.

And after you receive from God what you prayed for, still worship him.

JESUS CHRIST loves you more than what you know!!!!!!!